¡Qué chévere!

Second Edition

Level 1

Grammar and Vocabulary

Paul J. Hoff

Nuria Ibarrechevea Hoff

PITTSBURGH, PA

Publisher
Alex Vargas

Director of Content Development
Kristin Hoffman

Spanish Editor
Gustavo Vargas

Production Manager
Bob Dreas

Senior Designer & Production Specialist
Jaana Bykonich

ISBN 978-1-53384-994-6

501 Grant St.
Union Trust Building, Suite 1075
Pittsburgh, PA 15219
E-mail: info@carnegielearning.com
Web site: www.emcschool.com

Printed in the United States of America

28 27 26 25 24 23 22 5 6 7 8 9 10

Table of Contents

Nombre: ______________________________ Fecha: ______________

Unidad 1

Lección A

1 Complete the following conversation by choosing from the words in the box.

mucho	tú	hola	me	yo

CLARA: ¡Hola!

ANA: ¡(1) ____________________! ¿Cómo te llamas?

CLARA: (2) ____________________ llamo Clara. ¿Y (3) ____________________?

ANA: (4) ____________________ me llamo Ana.

CLARA: ¡(5) ____________________ gusto, Ana!

ANA: ¡Mucho gusto, Clara!

2 Write eight different Spanish first names. Each name should begin with the first letter of the country listed in the left column.

	País	Nombre
MODELO:	España	Esteban
1.	Colombia	____________________
2.	Ecuador	____________________
3.	México	____________________
4.	Panamá	____________________
5.	Guatemala	____________________
6.	Venezuela	____________________
7.	Argentina	____________________
8.	Nicaragua	____________________

Nombre: ______________________________ Fecha: ______________

3 The following Spanish first names have their letters in the wrong order. Spell the names correctly by starting with the capital letter and putting the other letters in their correct order. Then say the letters found in each name.

1. drePo ______________________________
2. Ddvia ______________________________
3. faíSo ______________________________
4. itCrsian ______________________________
5. qeRalu ______________________________
6. lMeuna ______________________________
7. sanSau ______________________________

4 Write the next numbers based on the sequence provided.

1. dos, cuatro, ______________, ______________, ______________
2. tres, seis, ______________, ______________, ______________
3. cuatro, ocho, ______________, ______________, ______________
4. quince, catorce, ______________, ______________, ______________
5. veinte, dieciocho, ______________, ______________, ______________

5 Find six numbers that are spelled out in the grid.

S	I	E	T	E	D	A
Z	O	Y	P	S	U	X
B	V	T	R	E	S	Z
O	E	L	U	N	O	W
C	I	N	C	O	S	Ñ
O	N	O	L	A	E	I
R	T	E	D	X	I	B
Q	E	V	W	K	S	G

Nombre: ______________________ Fecha: ____________

6 Complete each addition problem.

MODELO: 5 + 8 = trece

1. 9 + 6 = ____________
2. 2 + 5 = ____________
3. 11 + 9 = ____________
4. 10 + 2 = ____________
5. 16 + 3 = ____________
6. 4 + 10 = ____________

7 Match each country in the left column with its capital city in the right column.

1. ______ Chile		A. Santo Domingo
2. ______ Ecuador		B. San José
3. ______ Argentina		C. Caracas
4. ______ Paraguay		D. Montevideo
5. ______ España		E. Lima
6. ______ Cuba		F. Madrid
7. ______ Costa Rica		G. Santiago
8. ______ Venezuela		H. La Habana
9. ______ Puerto Rico		I. Buenos Aires
10. ______ Uruguay		J. Tegucigalpa
11. ______ Bolivia		K. San Juan
12. ______ República Dominicana		L. Asunción
13. ______ Honduras		M. La Paz
14. ______ Perú		N. Quito

Nombre: ______________________ Fecha: ____________

8 The preceding exercise lists fourteen countries and capitals. Now list five additional Spanish-speaking nations and their corresponding capital cities.

	País	Capital
1.	______________	______________
2.	______________	______________
3.	______________	______________
4.	______________	______________
5.	______________	______________

9 Answer the following questions in complete sentences in order to give your name, age and hometown or country of origin.

1. ¿Cómo te llamas?

   ____

2. ¿Cuántos años tienes?

   ____

3. ¿De dónde eres?

   ____

10 You just received the first text message from your new ePal. Read the information and answer the questions that follow.

Hola amigo/a, me llamo Jorge y tengo quince años. Soy de México y vivo en la capital. ¡Es muy grande! Estudio inglés y música. En mi opinión, ¡el inglés es fantástico! Saludos, Jorge

1. What is his name?

   ____

2. Where is he from?

   ____

3. How old is he?

   ____

4. Write at least one other thing you learn about this person

   ____

   ____

   ____

Nombre: ______________________________ Fecha: ______________

Lección B

1 Complete the conversation by choosing from the words in the box.

bien	cómo	**pronto**	estás	**estoy**	tú

CARLOS: ¡Hola! ¿Cómo (1)________________?

JUAN: (2)________________ regular, gracias. Y (3)________________, ¿qué tal?

CARLOS: Muy (4)________________, gracias.

2 You have learned a variety of greetings and farewells in Unit 1. Write an appropriate greeting or good-bye for each of the following situations.

1. You meet your friends at school in the morning.

   ____

2. You say good-bye to your Spanish teacher as you leave class.

   ____

3. You greet a friend at 3:00 in the afternoon.

   ____

4. You say good-bye to a friend you will see later in the day.

   ____

5. You greet your friends when you arrive at an evening event.

   ____

6. You say good night to a friend you will see tomorrow.

   ____

Nombre: ______________________________ Fecha: ______________

Repaso rápido: Informal and formal subject pronouns

In Spanish you should use the informal *tú* when talking to someone you refer to by a first name. Use the more formal *usted* (abbreviated *Ud.*) with an adult you don't know well or when speaking with someone you would address using a title such as *señor*, *señora* or *señorita*. In most Spanish-speaking countries the plural *ustedes* (abbreviated *Uds.*) is used when talking formally or informally to two or more people. However, in Spain people distinguish between the formal *ustedes* and the informal *vosotros/as*, which is used when speaking with two or more friends.

3 Indicate whether you should use *tú*, *Ud.*, *Uds.*, *vosotros* or *vosotras* with the following people.

1. your sister ______________
2. your dentist ______________
3. three friends in Mexico ______________
4. two female friends in Spain ______________
5. a group of teachers ______________
6. a salesperson in a store ______________
7. your friend in Chile ______________

4 Teresa is a very polite student. Write what she says in the following situations.

1. She asks a friend for help with her homework.

   ____

2. She interrupts a conversation in order to deliver a message.

   ____

3. She wants to pass through a line in the school cafeteria.

   ____

4. She responds to a friend who has thanked her for her assistance.

   ____

Nombre: ______________________________ Fecha: ______________

5 Complete each math problem.

MODELO: 15 + 20 = treinta y cinco

1. 12 + 30 = ______________
2. 28 + 37 = ______________
3. 60 + 18 = ______________
4. 55 - 22 = ______________
5. 93 - 40 = ______________
6. 100 - 86 = ______________
7. 3 x 20 = ______________

6 Complete the following chart. In the left column put the names of four different relatives. Then write their ages in digits and in words in the middle and right columns.

Nombre	Edad (en números)	Edad (en letras)
1.		
2.		
3.		
4.		

7 Write the missing number to complete each sequence.

1. cero, diez, veinte, ______________
2. cero, ocho, dieciséis, ______________
3. cero, ______________, treinta, cuarenta y cinco
4. cero, veinticuatro, ______________, setenta y dos
5. cero, treinta y uno, sesenta y dos, ______________
6. cero, veintisiete, ______________, ochenta y uno

Nombre: ______________________________ Fecha: ______________

Repaso rápido: Time

Remember the following expressions to ask for and to say what time it is:

What time is it?	It is (number) o'clock.
¿Qué hora es?	*Es la* (+ number)./*Son las* (+ number).

Use *y* (+ number of minutes through *veintinueve*) to add minutes after the hour or *menos* (+ number of minutes through *veintinueve*) to indicate time before the hour. Add *y cuarto* for a quarter past the hour, *y media* for half past the hour and *menos cuarto* for a quarter to the hour. Two additional useful expressions: *Es mediodía* (It is noon) and *Es medianoche* (It is midnight).

The expression A.M. is equivalent to *de la mañana* (in the morning) and P.M. is equivalent to *de la tarde* (in the afternoon) or to *de la noche* (at night).

8 Write the indicated times using complete sentences.

MODELO:  P.M. Son las siete y veinte de la noche.

1. 9:05 A.M. ______________________________

2. 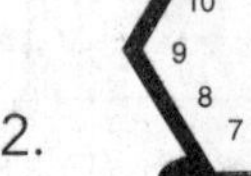 P.M. ______________________________

3.  P.M. ______________________________

4. 10:40 P.M. ______________________________

5.  A.M. ______________________________

Nombre: ______________________ Fecha: ____________

Unidad 2

Lección A

Repaso rápido: Subject pronouns and the verb *ser*

Remember that the verb *ser* is one of two Spanish verbs that mean **to be**.

yo	**soy**	*I am*	nosotros/nosotras	**somos**	*we are*
tú	**eres**	*you are*	vosotros/vosotras	**sois**	*you are*
Ud.		*you are*	Uds.		*you are*
él	**es**	*he (it) is*	ellos	**son**	*they are*
ella		*she (it) is*	ellas		*they are*

The verb *ser* has several different uses. For example, we use it to express origin and profession:

¿De dónde eres tú?	Where are you from?
Soy de California.	I am from California.
Enrique es profesor.	Enrique is a teacher.

1 Write the subject pronoun that refers to the people listed below.

1. Roberto ______________________
2. Susana ______________________
3. Carlos y Carolina ______________________
4. tú y yo______________________
5. Miguel y tú______________________
6. Elena y Gloria ______________________
7. Marta y Ud. ______________________

Nombre: ______________________________ Fecha: ______________

2 Match the subject pronoun in the left column with the corresponding form of the verb *ser* in the right column.

1. ______ Uds. | A. soy
2. ______ tú | B. somos
3. ______ Felipe | C. son
4. ______ yo | D. eres
5. ______ ellos | E. es
6. ______ nosotros

3 Use the correct form of the verb *ser* to complete the sentences below.

1. Nosotros ______________________ estudiantes de español.
2. Isabel Allende ______________________ escritora. Ella ______________________ de Chile.
3. Yo ______________________ de Estados Unidos. ¿De dónde ______________________ Uds.?
4. Tú ______________________ estudiante.
5. Frida Kahlo y Pablo Picasso ______________________ artistas.

4 Write three logical vocabulary words pertaining to your Spanish classroom for each category listed.

1. things on the wall

____

____

____

2. pieces of furniture

____

____

____

3. items you use to study

____

____

____

4. things that need electricity

____

____

____

Nombre: ______________________________ Fecha: ______________

Repaso rápido: Using definite articles with nouns

Nouns refer to people, places, things or concepts. All nouns in Spanish are either masculine or feminine. A masculine noun is often preceded by the definite article *el* while a feminine article is often accompanied by the definite article *la*.

el chico	*la chica*
el cuaderno	*la nación*
el papel	*la posibilidad*

Nouns that end in a vowel in Spanish are made plural by adding *-s*. Nouns that end in a consonant are made plural by adding *-es*. With plural nouns the definite articles become *los* and *las*.

la clase	→	*las clases*
el bolígrafo	→	*los bolígrafos*
el profesor	→	*los profesores*
la presentación	→	*las presentaciones*

5 Write the appropriate definite article for each noun.

1. ______profesora
2. ______reloj
3. ______libro
4. ______pared
5. ______puerta
6. ______bolígrafo
7. ______computadora
8. ______televisor

Nombre: ______________________________ Fecha: ______________

6 Change each article and noun to the plural form.

1. la puerta ______________________________
2. el mapa ______________________________
3. la estudiante ______________________________
4. la pizarra ______________________________
5. el pupitre ______________________________

7 Change each article and noun to the singular form.

1. las profesoras ______________________________
2. los libros ______________________________
3. los papeles ______________________________
4. las escuelas ______________________________
5. las sillas ______________________________

8 In the left column write the appropriate indefinite article for each noun. Then write the plural form of both the indefinite article and the noun in the right column.

Repaso rápido: Using indefinite articles with nouns

You have already learned the definite articles *el, la, los* and *las.* Nouns also may be preceded by the indefinite articles *un* or *una* (**a**, **an**, **one**) or the plural indefinite articles *unos* or *unas* (**some**, **a few**).

un chico *una chica* *unos libros* *unas revistas*

1. ______borrador ______________________________
2. ______puerta ______________________________
3. ______profesora ______________________________
4. ______mapa ______________________________
5. ______periódico ______________________________
6. ______ventana ______________________________

Nombre: ______________________________ Fecha: ______________

Lección B

1 Find five colors that are spelled out in the grid.

B	Y	Z	E	F	G	L
R	P	A	Z	U	L	C
O	T	P	O	I	M	V
J	N	E	G	R	O	E
O	P	O	Y	X	E	R
P	L	G	R	I	S	D
M	U	L	P	I	T	E

2 In the left column write the names of eight objects you find in your Spanish classroom. Then write the color of each item in the right column.

	Objeto	Color
MODELO:	la pizarra	blanca
1.	______________	______________
2.	______________	______________
3.	______________	______________
4.	______________	______________
5.	______________	______________
6.	______________	______________
7.	______________	______________
8.	______________	______________

Nombre: ______________________________ Fecha: ______________

3 Match each food or animal from the left column with its appropriate color(s).

Comidas y animales	Colores
1. ______ la banana	A. negro y blanco
2. ______ el tomate	B. verde
3. ______ el brócoli	C. gris
4. ______ el elefante	D. rojo
5. ______ el pingüino	E. amarillo

4 Put the days of the week in their correct order starting with Monday. Then indicate your preferences by numbering the days 1-7 with the number 1 corresponding to your favorite day.

sábado lunes jueves domingo martes miércoles viernes

	Día	Preferencia
1.	______________________	______
2.	______________________	______
3.	______________________	______
4.	______________________	______
5.	______________________	______
6.	______________________	______
7.	______________________	______

Nombre: ______________________ Fecha: __________

5 For each day of the week write the Spanish names for your classes.

lunes	martes	miércoles	jueves	viernes

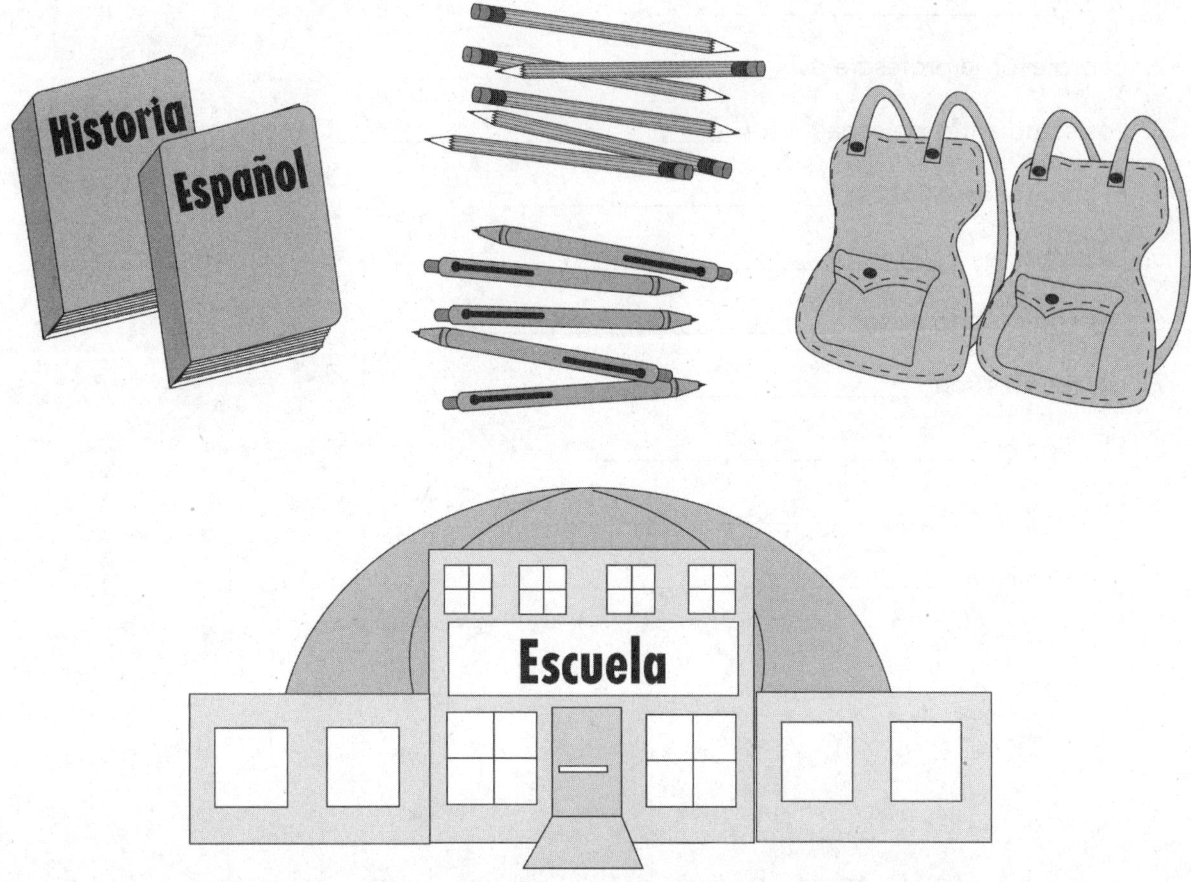

Nombre: ______________________________ Fecha: ______________

Repaso rápido: Using adjectives to describe

An adjective describes a noun or pronoun. In Spanish, adjectives must match the gender (masculine or feminine) and number (singular or plural) of the nouns they modify. As shown below, adjectives that end in *-o* have four different forms while adjectives that end in other letters have two different forms.

un papel blanco	→	*unos papeles blancos*
una mesa blanca	→	*unas mesas blancas*
un libro verde	→	*unos libros verdes*
una mochila verde	→	*unas mochilas verdes*
un cuaderno azul	→	*unos cuadernos azules*
una silla azul	→	*unas sillas azules*

6 Choose from the adjectives listed below to complete the following sentences in a logical fashion. Be sure that each adjective agrees with the noun that it modifies.

rojo	tímido	negro	amarillo	gris
activo	inteligente	cómico	serio	azul
verde	honesto	importante	interesante	blanco

1. Yo soy ______________________.
2. El profesor/la profesora es ______________________.
3. Los estudiantes de español son ______________________.
4. El libro de español es ______________________.
5. La pizarra es ______________________.
6. Las computadoras son ______________________.
7. Las revistas son ______________________.
8. El mapa es ______________________.
9. Mis amigos son ______________________.
10. Mi mochila es ______________________.

Nombre: ______________________ Fecha: __________

7 Put the names of six friends in the left column and then choose from the adjectives found in the previous activity to describe them. Be sure that each adjective agrees with the person it describes.

	Nombre	**Descripción**
MODELO:	Luisa	Luisa es activa.
1.	______________	______________
2.	______________	______________
3.	______________	______________
4.	______________	______________
5.	______________	______________
6.	______________	______________

8 Choose from the adjectives in the box and use the correct form of the verb *ser* to describe the classes listed below.

interesante popular importante imposible fantástico complicado

1. La historia ______________.
2. La biología ______________.
3. Las matemáticas ______________.
4. La música ______________.
5. El arte ______________.
6. El español ______________.
7. El inglés ______________.

Nombre: ______________________ Fecha: ______________

Repaso rápido: Present tense of *-ar* verbs

Verbs express an action or a state of being. The infinitive form of a verb in Spanish will end with *-ar*, *-er* or *-ir*. For example, *hablar* means to speak and *estudiar* means to study. To form the present tense of regular *-ar* verbs, remove the *-ar* ending and then attach the appropriate ending as shown below.

yo	habl**o**	nosotros nosotras	habl**amos**
tú	habl**as**	vosotros vosotras	habl**áis**
Ud. él ella	habl**a**	Uds. ellos ellas	habl**an**

9 Choose the appropriate infinitive and then write the correct present-tense verb form to complete each sentence.

estudiar hablar necesitar terminar

1. Yo ______________________ un cuaderno nuevo.
2. Tú ______________________ mucho por teléfono.
3. Clara ______________________ arte y matemáticas.
4. Los estudiantes ______________________ las clases a las tres de la tarde.
5. Marcos ______________________ el libro de biología.
6. El profesor ______________________ español en la clase.
7. Mis amigos y yo ______________________ lápices de color para la clase de arte.
8. Uds. ______________________ la clase temprano (*early*).
9. Juan y tú no ______________________ mucho para el examen.

Nombre: ______________________________ Fecha: ______________

10 Complete the following sentences logically, using the correct present-tense forms of the verbs in parentheses and any additional words necessary.

MODELO: Ellos llevan unos zapatos negros. (llevar)

1. Los estudiantes ______________________________. (hablar)
2. La clase de español ______________________________. (terminar)
3. Nosotros ______________________________. (estudiar)
4. Los profesores ______________________________. (necesitar)

Repaso rápido: ¿A qúe hora?

¿A qué hora…? asks the time of a given event. To state when something takes place, use *es a la/las...*; to state when something ends, use *termina a la/las….*

11 Based on the classes you study, answer as many of the following questions as possible.

1. ¿A qué hora es la clase de español?

____

2. ¿A qué hora es la clase de educación física?

____

3. ¿A qué hora es la clase de inglés?

____

4. ¿A qué hora termina la clase de matemáticas?

____

5. ¿A qué hora termina la clase de biología?

____

6. ¿A qué hora termina la clase de música?

____

Nombre: ______________________ Fecha: __________

12 Your family has asked you to organize a new office in your home. List five basic supplies and five computer-related items that you will need.

	Para la oficina necesito:	**Para la computadora necesito:**
1.	______________	______________
2.	______________	______________
3.	______________	______________
4.	______________	______________
5.	______________	______________

13 Write down four phone numbers you call regularly and spell them out. Then state with whom you speak in each instance.

MODELO: Número de teléfono: 7-52-31-16
siete, cincuenta y dos, treinta y uno, dieciséis
Persona: Hablo con Esteban.

1. Número de teléfono: ______________________

   ____

   Persona: ______________________
2. Número de teléfono: ______________________

   ____

   Persona: ______________________
3. Número de teléfono: ______________________

   ____

   Persona: ______________________
4. Número de teléfono: ______________________

   ____

   Persona: ______________________

Nombre: ______________________________ Fecha: ______________

Repaso rápido: *Estar*

The verb *estar* (to be) is irregular in the present tense.

yo	**estoy**	nosotros nosotras	**estamos**
tú	**estás**	vosotros vosotras	**estáis**
Ud. él ella	**está**	Uds. ellos ellas	**están**

As shown in the following examples, *estar* is used to express location and states of being or conditions.

¿Dónde está Cuernavaca?
Cuernavaca está en México.

¿Cómo está Ud.?
Estoy regular.

14 Say how you and others feel in the following locations by using the correct form of the verb *estar* and choosing from the following expressions: *muy bien, bien, regular, mal, muy mal.*

1. En el colegio yo ______________________________.
2. En la clase de español nosotros ______________________________.
3. En la clase de español el profesor/la profesora ______________________________.
4. En la clase de matemáticas los estudiantes ______________________________.
5. En una fiesta Rosa ______________________________.
6. En la cafetería tú ______________________________.

Nombre: ______________________________ Fecha: ______________

15 Use the correct form of the verb *estar* and your knowledge of the Spanish-speaking world to answer the following questions.

1. ¿Dónde está Barcelona?

   ____

2. ¿Dónde está San Juan?

   ____

3. ¿Dónde están Los Ángeles y San Diego?

   ____

4. ¿Dónde está Caracas?

   ____

5. ¿Dónde están Lima y Arequipa?

   ____

6. ¿Dónde está San José?

   ____

16 Answer the following questions about yourself and your school.

1. ¿Cómo se llama el colegio? ¿Dónde está?

   ____

2. ¿Qué ropa llevas en un día típico?

   ____

3. ¿Cuál es tu número de teléfono?

   ____

4. ¿Qué estudias?

   ____

5. ¿A qué hora es tu clase de español? ¿Qué necesitas en la clase?

   ____

Nombre: ______________________________ Fecha: ______________

Unidad 3

Lección A

1 Find six city locations that are spelled out in the grid.

F	B	O	P	U	Y	Z	E
P	A	H	O	T	E	L	S
I	N	Z	T	U	P	B	C
F	C	I	N	E	P	N	U
Y	O	L	C	E	O	T	E
O	P	A	R	Q	U	E	L
P	O	C	Y	T	R	B	A
M	O	F	I	C	I	N	A

2 Match each location in a city from the left column with a logical item in the right column.

1. ______ el banco
2. ______ el restaurante
3. ______ el cine
4. ______ el hotel
5. ______ la escuela
6. ______ el médico
7. ______ la oficina
8. ______ la biblioteca

A. papeles y cuadernos
B. dólares y pesos
C. estudiantes y profesores
D. sandwiches
E. aspirina
F. actores famosos
G. turistas
H. libros

Nombre: ______________________________ Fecha: ______________

Repaso rápido: Making introductions

Remember to use *te presento* to introduce someone informally and *le presento* when you want to be more formal. Use *les presento* to introduce two or more people.

*Ana, **te presento** a Javier.*
*Sra. Marcos, **le presento** a Teresa.*
*Manuel y Natalia, **les presento** a Pedro.*

There are two contractions in Spanish that involve the definite article *el*: *a + el = al*; *de + el = del*. These contractions often are used when speaking about a man with a certain title:

*Nacho, te presento **al** señor Ramírez.*
*Es el libro **del** profesor Sánchez.*

but:

*Nacho, te presento **a la** señora Ramírez y **a los** señores López.*
*El libro es **de la** profesora Iglesias.*

When you are introduced to someone, there are several ways to respond. They include *Mucho gusto, Tanto gusto, El gusto es mío* and *Encantado/Encantada*.

3 Complete the following dialog in an informal manner.

RAFAEL: Carmen, (1) ____________________ presento a mi amigo Francisco.

CARMEN: (2) ____________________ gusto, Francisco.

FRANCISCO: (3) ____________________. ¿Cómo (4) ____________________?

CARMEN: Bien, gracias. ¿Y (5) ____________________?

FRANCISCO: Muy (6) ____________________, gracias.

Nombre: ________________________________ Fecha: ______________

4 Complete the following dialog in a formal manner.

PILAR: Sr. Durán, (1) ____________________ presento a María.

SR. DURÁN: Mucho (2) ____________________, María.

MARÍA: El gusto (3) ____________________ mío.

¿Cómo (4) ____________________ Ud.?

SR. DURÁN: Bien, gracias. ¿Y (5) ____________________?

MARÍA: (6) ____________________ bien.

5 Complete each sentence in an appropriate fashion, choosing from the words *al*, *a la*, *a los*, *a las*, *del*, *de la*, *de los* and *de las*.

1. La clase ____________________ profesora Torres es excelente.
2. Las clases ____________________ señor Mejía son interesantes.
3. Aquí están los papeles ____________________ señores Peralta.
4. Señora Donoso, le presento ____________________ profesor Gómez.
5. Susana, te presento ____________________ señora Ortiz.
6. Mercedes y Marta, les presento ____________________ señores Gómez.

6 Choose the appropriate word(s) to complete each question.

1. ¿Dónde / Cómo está el restaurante?
2. ¿Por qué / Dónde van ellos al parque?
3. ¿Cuáles / A qué hora es la clase?
4. ¿Qué / Cuál es el número de teléfono de Sofía?
5. ¿Cuántos / Cuándo hay una fiesta fantástica?
6. ¿Quién / Dónde es de Cancún?
7. ¿Cómo / Cuáles están los estudiantes?
8. ¿Cuándo / Quién es la amiga de Jorge?

Nombre: ______________________________ Fecha: ______________

Repaso rápido: Asking questions

In addition to asking questions with interrogative words, it is important to be able to ask yes-no questions. There are several ways to do so in Spanish:

- Use a rising tone as you speak. *¿Paco estudia español?*
- Place the subject after the verb. *¿Está Paco en la clase?*
- Use the tag question *¿no?* or *¿verdad?* *Paco estudia música, ¿verdad?*

7 Change the following statements to questions by placing the subjects after the verbs and by using tag questions.

MODELO: Alejandro habla inglés y español.
¿Habla Alejandro inglés y español?
Alejandro habla inglés y español, ¿no?
Alejandro habla inglés y español, ¿verdad?

1. Los estudiantes son de Bolivia.

____

____

2. Ellos están en la fiesta.

____

____

3. Lola tiene quince años.

____

____

4. Lola y Eduardo son muy activos.

____

____

5. Eduardo termina la clase a las tres.

____

____

Nombre: ______________________ Fecha: ____________

8 Complete the following questions by inserting the appropriate question words. Remember that all interrogative words require a written accent.

1. ¿ ______________ te llamas?
2. ¿ De ______________ eres?
3. ¿ ______________ años tienes?
4. ¿ ______________ estás?
5. Hay muchas clases en la escuela. ¿ ______________ es una clase muy interesante?
6. ¿ ______________ estudiantes hay en la clase de español?
7. ¿A ______________ hora es la clase de español?
8. ¿ ______________ está el profesor/la profesora de español?
9. ¿ ______________ es una persona famosa de México?

9 In the preceding exercise you formulated nine questions. Now answer each question in a complete sentence.

1. ______________________________
2. ______________________________
3. ______________________________
4. ______________________________
5. ______________________________
6. ______________________________
7. ______________________________
8. ______________________________
9. ______________________________

Nombre: ______________________________ Fecha: ______________

10 Fill in the missing question words in the following dialog.

DIANA: ¡Hola Pablo! ¿(1) ______________ estás?

PABLO: Muy bien, Diana. ¿Y tú?

DIANA: Bien. ¿A (2) ______________ hora es la fiesta de Paco?

PABLO: La fiesta es mañana a las ocho.

DIANA: ¿(3) ______________ está la casa de Paco?

PABLO: La casa está en el centro. ¿(4) ______________ años tiene Paco?

DIANA: Quince. ¡Y mañana dieciséis!

PABLO: Bueno, hasta mañana.

DIANA: Adiós.

Nombre: ______________________________ Fecha: ______________

Repaso rápido: *Ir*

The verb *ir* (to go) is irregular in the present tense. It is generally followed by the preposition *a* (or the contraction *al*) and a destination.

yo	**voy**	nosotros nosotras	**vamos**
tú	**vas**	vosotros vosotras	**vais**
Ud. él ella	**va**	Uds. ellos ellas	**van**

Yo voy a la fiesta y Luisa va a la oficina.
Marcos y Rosa van al restaurante.

11 Form complete sentences with the information provided and adding any necessary words.

MODELO: yo / ir / Puerto Rico / barco
Yo voy a Puerto Rico en barco.

1. Carlos / ir / escuela / carro

____

2. nosotros / ir / supermercado / autobús

____

3. tú / ir / cine / taxi

____

4. Tomás y Sofía / ir / biblioteca / pie

____

5. Ud. / ir / café / bicicleta

____

6. yo / ir / Chile / avión

____

Nombre: ______________________________ Fecha: ______________

12 Match each subject in the left column with the appropriate form of the verb *ir* in the right column.

1. ______ nosotros	A. vas
2. ______ Lola	B. voy
3. ______ Uds.	C. vamos
4. ______ yo	D. vais
5. ______ tú	E. va
6. ______ Ud.	F. van

13 Combine items from each column in order to write eight logical sentences. Remember that *a* + *el* = *al*.

yo		la clase
tú		la oficina
Ud.		el parque
Felipe	ir + a	el restaurante
Elena		la fiesta
nosotros		la escuela
los estudiantes		el banco
los profesores		el hotel

1. ______________________________

2. ______________________________

3. ______________________________

4. ______________________________

5. ______________________________

6. ______________________________

7. ______________________________

8. ______________________________

Nombre: ______________________________ Fecha: ______________

Lección B

1 Use the verb *ir* and the illustrations to say where the following people are going.

MODELO:  Yo voy al centro.

1.  Nosotros ______________________________.

2.  Los chicos ______________________________.

3.  Yo ______________________________.

4. 

Gloria ______________________________.

5.  Tú ______________________________.

6. 

Ud. ______________________________.

Nombre: ______________________________ Fecha: ______________

2 Match each location in a city from the left column with a logical item from the right column.

1. ______ el museo
2. ______ el restaurante mexicano
3. ______ la calle
4. ______ las tiendas
5. ______ el teatro
6. ______ el hospital

A. libros, televisores y más
B. enchiladas
C. médicos, pacientes, medicina
D. historia y arte
E. carros y autobuses
F. conciertos

Repaso rápido: *Ir a* + infinitive

To say what is going to happen in the future, use the present tense of the verb *ir*, followed by *a* and an infinitive.

Yo voy a ser artista. *Nosotros vamos a ir al teatro.*

3 Combine items from the columns to write statements about what is going to happen.

yo		hablar por teléfono
tú		caminar en el parque
Claudia	ir a	estudiar en la biblioteca
Ud.		ir al restaurante
los profesores		tomar el autobús
María y yo		ir en bicicleta por el parque

1. ______________________________
2. ______________________________
3. ______________________________
4. ______________________________
5. ______________________________
6. ______________________________

Nombre: ______________________ Fecha: ____________

4 Imagine that you are planning a trip to different Spanish-speaking countries. Write five cities or countries you are going to visit and something you are going to do in each one.

MODELO: Voy a ir a México. En México voy a ir a los museos.

1. ______________________
2. ______________________
3. ______________________
4. ______________________
5. ______________________

5 Choose from the list of professions to make eight predictions about what you and your classmates are going to be in the future.

banquero/a	ingeniero/a	profesor(a)	dentista
médico/a	mecánico/a	intérprete	programador(a)
científico/a	sicólogo/a	astronauta	diplomático/a
artista	fotógrafo/a	recepcionista	político/a
agente de viajes	mujer de negocios	hombre de negocios	sociólogo/a

	Nombre	Futuro
MODELO:	Clara	Clara va a ser artista.
1.	____________	____________
2.	____________	____________
3.	____________	____________
4.	____________	____________
5.	____________	____________
6.	____________	____________
7.	____________	____________
8.	____________	____________

Nombre: ______________________ Fecha: __________

6 You have been asked to prepare the menu for two meals. Fill in the foods of your choice but do not list any item more than once.

	Menú 1	Menú 2
• Entrada *(first course)*	______________	______________
• Plato principal *(main course)*	______________	______________
• Bebida *(beverage)*	______________	______________

7 Combine information from each column in a logical fashion to form sentences. As you do so, pay special attention to using the *-ar* verbs correctly.

yo	necesitar	unos *jeans*
los estudiantes	estudiar	una computadora nueva
la profesora	hablar	arte y biología
nosotros	llevar	a las tres y cuarto
tú	terminar	español en la clase

1. ______________________________
2. ______________________________
3. ______________________________
4. ______________________________
5. ______________________________

Nombre: ______________________ Fecha: ______________

Repaso rápido: Present tense of *-er* verbs

To form the present tense of regular *-er* verbs, first remove the *-er* ending and then attach the endings that correspond to each of the subject pronouns.

yo	com**o**	nosotros nosotras	com**emos**
tú	com**es**	vosotros vosotras	com**éis**
Ud. él ella	com**e**	Uds. ellos ellas	com**en**

Remember that the verbs *hacer, ver* and *saber* are conjugated like *comer* except for the *yo* forms.

hacer → yo **hago**
ver → yo **veo**
saber → yo **sé**

8 Choose from the three infinitives in the box and then write the appropriate verb form to complete each sentence.

comer **comprender** leer

1. Las chicas ______________________ en el restaurante.
2. Nosotros ______________________ el periódico.
3. Tú ______________________ las matemáticas.
4. Yo ______________________ el libro de español.
5. Patricia ______________________ una ensalada verde.
6. Uds. ______________________ el problema.
7. Ud. ______________________ la revista.

Nombre: ______________________ Fecha: ____________

9 Answer the following questions about your food and beverage preferences.

1. ¿Tomas agua mineral?

____

2. ¿Cómo se llama tu refresco favorito?

____

3. ¿Cómo se llama tu restaurante favorito?

____

4. ¿Qué comes en tu restaurante favorito?

____

5. ¿Cuál es tu comida favorita?

____

10 Use the following questions to interview a classmate about his/her food and beverage preferences. When you are done you should be ready to report several pieces of information to the class.

1. ¿Tomas jugo de naranja?

____

2. ¿Tomas agua mineral?

____

3. ¿Cómo se llama tu refresco favorito?

____

4. ¿Cómo se llama tu restaurante favorito?

____

5. ¿Qué comes en tu restaurante favorito?

____

6. ¿Cuál es tu comida favorita?

____

Nombre: ______________________________ Fecha: ______________

11 Friends often have much in common. Read each statement and then note that someone else does the same thing.

MODELO: David ve la televisión. (nosotros)
Nosotros vemos la televisión también.

1. Marta sabe la información. (tú)

   ____

2. Roberto y Lupe hacen muchas preguntas. (yo)

   ____

3. Yo como pollo con mole. (nosotros)

   ____

4. Los estudiantes comprenden la situación. (Luisa)

   ____

5. Antonio ve el programa. (yo)

   ____

6. Pedro lee el periódico. (Carolina y Javier)

   ____

7. Ellos saben cuál es la capital de México. (yo)

   ____

8. Tú ves mucha comida buena en el menú. (yo)

   ____

9. Ana comprende la lección de matemáticas. (los estudiantes)

   ____

10. Mamá lee el revista. (yo)

   ____

Nombre: ____ Fecha: ______________

12 Answer the following personalized questions in complete sentences.

1. ¿Qué revistas lees?

   ____

2. ¿Qué programas ves en la televisión?

   ____

3. ¿Qué tomas por la mañana?

   ____

4. ¿Qué comes en un restaurante mexicano?

   ____

5. ¿Sabes cuál es la capital de México?

   ____

6. ¿Haces muchas o pocas preguntas en clase?

   ____

7. ¿Comprendes bien el español?

   ____

8. ¿Tomas muchos refrescos?

   ____

9. ¿Ves televisión a las nueve de la noche?

   ____

10. ¿Sabes muchas palabras en español?

   ____

Nombre: ______________________________ Fecha: ______________

Unidad 4

Lección A

1 Complete each statement with the appropriate family member.

1. El hermano de mi madre es mi ____________________.
2. La madre de mi madre es mi ____________________.
3. La hija de mis tíos es mi ____________________.
4. La esposa de mi tío es mi ____________________.
5. El esposo de mi abuela es mi ____________________.
6. La hija de mis padres es mi ____________________.
7. La hija de mi hermana es mi ____________________.
8. Yo, Ana, soy la ____________________ de mis abuelos.
9. Mis hermanos y yo somos los ____________________ de nuestros padres.
10. Mi madre es la ____________________ de mi padre.

2 In the left column put the names of six different relatives. Then explain the relationship of each one to you.

	Pariente	**Relación**
MODELO:	Ana	Ana es mi hermana.
1.	____________________	______________________________
2.	____________________	______________________________
3.	____________________	______________________________
4.	____________________	______________________________
5.	____________________	______________________________
6.	____________________	______________________________

Nombre: ______________________________ Fecha: ______________

3 Answer the questions about the family tree.

Nombre: ______________________________ Fecha: ______________

1. ¿Cómo se llama el padre de Rosita?

____

2. ¿Cómo se llaman las abuelas de Humberto?

____

3. ¿Cómo se llama el hermano de Carlos?

____

4. ¿Cómo se llaman los tíos de Hilda?

____

5. ¿Cómo se llama el esposo de Ana?

____

6. ¿Cómo se llaman las primas de Humberto?

____

4 Answer the following questions about your family in complete sentences.

1. ¿Cuántos hermanos tienes?

____

2. ¿Cuántos primos tienes?

____

3. ¿Cuántos tíos tienes?

____

4. ¿Cuántas personas viven en tu casa? ¿Quiénes son?

____

____

5. ¿Quién es tu pariente favorito?

____

Nombre: ______________________________ Fecha: ______________

5 Complete the following sentences with the correct form of the adjectives shown in parentheses. Pay special attention to the agreement of gender and number.

1. Tengo ____________________ amigos. (mucho)
2. Mi hermana es ____________________. (divertido)
3. Nosotros estudiamos ____________________ los días. (todo)
4. Mis primos son ____________________. (popular)
5. Vivimos en una casa ____________________. (blanco)
6. Tengo una tía en Miami y ____________________ tía en San Diego. (otro)
7. Mis abuelas son muy ____________________. (cariñoso)

6 Think of a family member who is very special to you. Put the name of this relative in the blank and then write five statements to describe her/him. As you do so, be sure to include different types of information you have learned to express in Spanish. Pay special attention to verb conjugations and adjective agreement.

Nombre: ______________________________

1. ______________________________
2. ______________________________
3. ______________________________
4. ______________________________
5. ______________________________

Nombre: ______________________________ Fecha: ______________

Repaso rápido: Possessive adjectives

You can indicate possession by using the possessive adjectives. They precede the noun they modify and must agree in number and gender with that noun.

mi(s)	primo(s) prima(s)	**nuestro(s)** **nuestra(s)**	primo(s) prima(s)
tu(s)	hermano(s) hermana(s)	**vuestro(s)** **vuestra(s)**	hermano(s) hermana(s)
su(s)	tío(s) tía(s)	**su(s)**	tío(s) tía(s)
su(s)	tío(s) tía(s)	**su(s)**	tío(s) tía(s)
su(s)	tío(s) tía(s)		

Possessive adjectives have both singular and plural forms. In the following cases they also have different masculine and feminine forms: *nuestro/nuestra, nuestros/nuestras, vuestro/vuestra, vuestros/vuestras.* Remember that the possessive adjective agrees with what is possessed, not the possessor.

Mis tíos viven en Puerto Rico.	My aunt and uncle live in Puerto Rico.
Su casa está en San Juan.	Their house is in San Juan.

7 Provide the correct possessive adjective to complete each sentence.

MODELO: Nosotros tenemos una casa bonita. Nuestra casa está en San Juan.

1. Yo tengo seis primos. ______________________ primos son interesantes.
2. Susana tiene una hermana. ______________________ hermana se llama Dolores.
3. Tú tienes una familia grande. ______________________ familia tiene ocho personas.
4. Las hermanas de Marcos son inteligentes. ______________________ hermanas estudian mucho.
5. Uds. tienen una casa elegante. ______________________ casa es blanca y azul.
6. Nosotros tenemos muchos tíos. ______________________ tíos son divertidos.

Nombre: ______________________________ Fecha: ______________

Repaso rápido: Present tense of *-ir* verbs

To form the present tense of regular *-ir* verbs, first remove the *-ir* ending and then attach the endings that correspond to each of the subject pronouns.

yo	viv**o**	nosotros nosotras	viv**imos**
tú	viv**es**	vosotros vosotras	viv**ís**
Ud. él ella	viv**e**	Uds. ellos ellas	viv**en**

Remember that the verb *salir* is regular in all forms except the first person singular: *Yo salgo.*

8 Rosa lives in the United States but has relatives in several other countries. Take the role of Rosa and combine information from the three columns to say where different people live.

yo		Panamá
mi abuela María		Estados Unidos
mis primos Carlos y David		España
mi prima Susana	vivir en	Chile
mi tía Mercedes		Venezuela
mis padres y yo		Colombia
mis tíos José y Carmen		Bolivia

MODELO: Yo vivo en Estados Unidos.

1. ______________________________
2. ______________________________
3. ______________________________
4. ______________________________
5. ______________________________
6. ______________________________

Nombre: ______________________ Fecha: ____________

9 Take the role of Rosa to say at what time different people leave in the morning.

yo		
mi abuela María		a las seis
mis primos Carlos y David		a las siete
mi prima Susana	salir	a las siete y media
mi tía Mercedes		a las ocho
mis padres y yo		a las ocho y cuarto
mis tíos José y Carmen		

MODELO: Mi abuela María sale a las siete.

1. ______________________
2. ______________________
3. ______________________
4. ______________________
5. ______________________
6. ______________________

Repaso rápido: Describing people and things with *estar*

The verb *estar* is used with adjectives to describe certain conditions or states of being and to give observations at a given moment.

Francisco está nervioso.	Francisco is nervous.
Teresa está triste pero sus hermanos están contentos.	Teresa is sad but her brothers are happy.
Felipe está muy guapo hoy.	Felipe looks very nice today.

10 Say how the following people are feeling or looking today based on the information provided. In each case you should use a form of the verb *estar* and an appropriate adjective.

1. Marta tiene una temperatura de 102. Ella ______________________.
2. Clara y Ana tienen una "A" en sus exámenes. Ellas ______________________.
3. Tenemos tres exámenes importantes. Nosotros ______________________.
4. Mi abuela está enferma. Yo ______________________.
5. Natalia tiene una fiesta formal hoy. Ella ______________________.

Nombre: ______________________________ Fecha: ______________

11 Think of your house in a typical afternoon when you return home from school. Based on this image, complete the following sentences in a logical fashion by using the verb *estar* and adjectives from the box.

cerrado	caliente	limpio	sucio	libre
ocupado	frío	triste	cansado	
contento	abierto	apurado		

1. La casa ______________________________.
2. La puerta ______________________________.
3. El teléfono ______________________________.
4. Los refrescos ______________________________.
5. Yo ______________________________.

12 Your friend Rosa is on vacation, and she sent you a text message. Read her message and then answer the following questions in complete sentences in Spanish.

1. ¿Dónde está Rosa?

   ____

2. ¿Cómo está ella?

   ____

3. ¿Quién es Samuel?

   ____

4. ¿Dónde vive él?

   ____

5. ¿A qué hora sale el autobus para ir a San Juan?

   ____

Nombre: ______________________________ Fecha: ______________

Lección B

1 Find six activities that are spelled out in the grid.

C	O	P	I	N	S	T
O	N	A	D	A	R	M
M	D	V	O	I	R	I
P	O	E	L	E	A	R
R	Y	R	D	O	I	A
A	J	U	G	A	R	R
R	C	A	N	T	A	R

2 Match the activity in the left column with an item in the right column.

1. ______ jugar al béisbol	A. las clases
2. ______ patinar	B. el bate
3. ______ cantar	C. el programa
4. ______ comprar	D. la raqueta
5. ______ jugar al tenis	E. el concierto
6. ______ nadar	F. las fotos
7. ______ ver la televisión	G. la tienda
8. hacer la tarea	H. el piano
9. ______ mirar	I. el parque
10. ______ tocar	J. la playa

Nombre: ______________________ Fecha: ____________

Repaso rápido: Using *gustar* to state likes and dislikes

To express the idea of liking in Spanish use the verb *gustar*, which is similar to the English expression **to be pleasing**. The most commonly used forms of the verb *gustar* in the present tense are *gusta* and *gustan*.

Gusta is used with a singular noun or an infinitive while *gustan* is used with plural nouns. The indirect object pronoun that precedes the verb indicates who is pleased. To express dislike instead of like, put the word *no* before the indirect object pronoun.

me	*Me gusta el parque.*	I like the park.
te	*Te gusta la cafetería.*	You like the cafeteria.
nos	*Nos gusta el restaurante.*	We like the restaurant.

but:

No me gusta caminar en el parque. I don't like to walk in the park.

The verb *gustar* may also be preceded by *le* or *les*. Use *le* when speaking to someone formally or when talking about what another person likes or dislikes. Use *les* when speaking to or about two or more people.

¿Le gusta jugar al béisbol?	Do you (*Ud.*) like to play baseball?
Les gustan las clases.	You (*Uds.*) like the classes.

3 Answer each of the following questions in order to express your likes and dislikes.

1. ¿Te gusta el béisbol?

   ____

2. ¿Te gusta el básquetbol?

   ____

3. ¿Te gustan los museos?

   ____

4. ¿Te gustan los conciertos de rock?

   ____

Nombre: ______________________ Fecha: ____________

4 Choose from the following activities to write four statements about things you like to do and four statements about things you dislike.

comer en la cafetería	ir a restaurantes	leer el periódico
ver la televisión	estar en casa	tomar el autobús
salir con amigos	ir de compras	estudiar matemáticas

1. ______________________
2. ______________________
3. ______________________
4. ______________________
5. ______________________
6. ______________________
7. ______________________
8. ______________________

5 Friends often enjoy the same activities. Write six statements to explain what you and your friends like to do. Then write two statements about what you and your friends dislike doing.

MODELO: Nos gusta ir de compras.

1. ______________________
2. ______________________
3. ______________________
4. ______________________
5. ______________________
6. ______________________
7. ______________________
8. ______________________

Nombre: ______________________________ Fecha: ______________

6 Write what the following people like or like to do, according to the cues. Follow the models.

MODELO: Pedro (tocar el piano)
Le gusta tocar el piano.

Jaime y Pilar (los libros de Stephen King)
Les gustan los libros de Stephen King.

1. Rafael (jugar al tenis)

 ____

2. Marisol (los frijoles)

 ____

3. Tomás y Sofía (ver la televisión)

 ____

4. Samuel (el pescado)

 ____

5. Diego y Lyda (los refrescos de naranja)

 ____

6. Mi madre (los carros nuevos)

 ____

7. El primo de Julia (ir de compras)

 ____

8. Los estudiantes de español (hacer las tareas)

 ____

9. La profesora de matemáticas (las calculadoras buenas)

 ____

10. Las tías (la ropa moderna)

 ____

Nombre: ______________________ Fecha: ______________

Repaso rápido: Using *a* to clarify or emphasize what you are saying

The phrases listed below can be added to a sentence with *gustar* for clarity or emphasis.

A mí *me gusta nadar.*	***A nosotros (nosotras)*** *nos gusta nadar.*
A ti *te gusta nadar.*	***A vosotros (vosotras)*** *os gusta nadar.*
A Ud. *le gusta nadar.*	***A Uds.*** *les gusta nadar.*
A él (a Pablo/al profesor) *le gusta nadar.*	***A ellos (a Pablo y a Carlos)*** *les gusta nadar.*
A ella (a Teresa/a la profesora) *le gusta nadar.*	***A ellas (a Isabel y a Ana)*** *les gusta nadar.*

7 Combine words from each column to form seven original sentences.

a Ud.			hacer la tarea
a nosotros	me		ver la televisión
a mi amigo	te	gusta	ir en bicicleta
a mí	le	gustan	la playa
a los profesores	nos		los museos
a ti	les		las fotos
a mi tía			la escuela

1. ______________________________
2. ______________________________
3. ______________________________
4. ______________________________
5. ______________________________
6. ______________________________
7. ______________________________

Nombre: ________________________ Fecha: ____________

8 Use the cues to write six complete sentences.

MODELO: nosotros / gustar / leer revistas
<u>A nosotros nos gusta leer revistas.</u>

1. Uds. / gustar / escuchar la radio

____

2. Luisa / gustar / patinar sobre ruedas

____

3. tú / gustar / los conciertos de rock

____

4. Francisco / gustar / la comida mexicana

____

5. yo / gustar / las clases de música

____

6. nosotros / gustar / ir de compras

____

9 Answer the following questions about your likes/dislikes and those of your family members.

1. ¿Te gusta tocar el piano?

____

2. ¿A Uds. les gusta la música clásica?

____

3. ¿A quién le gusta la música rock?

____

4. ¿Te gusta jugar al tenis?

____

5. ¿A Uds. les gusta nadar?

____

Nombre: ______________________ Fecha: ____________

10 Describe the following people. Use at least two adjectives per description.

1. yo ______________________
2. mi amigo/a favorito/a ______________________
3. mi profesor(a) favorito/a ______________________
4. mis amigos ______________________
5. mis primos ______________________
6. el presidente de EE.UU. ______________________

11 Tomás and David are exact opposites. Read the descriptions of Tomás and then write statements about David.

MODELO: Tomás es alto. David es bajo.

1. Tomás es bueno. ______________________
2. Tomás es gordo. ______________________
3. Tomás es inteligente. ______________________
4. Tomás es feo. ______________________
5. Tomás es moreno. ______________________
6. Tomás es divertido. ______________________

Nombre: ______________________________ Fecha: ______________

Repaso rápido: *Ser* vs. *estar*

You already have learned that the English verb **to be** has two equivalents in Spanish: *ser* and *estar*.

The uses of *ser* include the following:

- to express origin — *Ellas son de Puerto Rico.*
- to express a basic characteristic or trait — *Mi hermana es baja y delgada.*
- to give the location of an event — *El concierto es en el teatro.*

The uses of *estar* include the following:

- to express a temporary condition or state — *Estoy triste pero Susana está bien.*
- to give the location of someone or something — *Alex está en su casa.* *Caracas está en Venezuela.*

12 Give the correct form of *ser* or *estar* to complete each sentence.

1. La Sra. Sosa ______________ de la República Dominicana.
2. Su casa ______________ en Santo Domingo pero ahora ella ______________ en España con sus hijos.
3. Ella ______________ inteligente y sus hijos ______________ altos.
4. Sus hijos ______________ contentos porque van a un concierto.
5. El concierto ______________ en el parque.

13 Write a paragraph of at least four sentences to describe yourself. In your description include your name and information about your origin, likes and dislikes, personality and appearance.

____

____

____

____

____

____

Nombre: ______________________________ Fecha: ______________

Unidad 5

Lección A

1 Choose the things below that you have and/or use in your home. Then answer the corresponding questions for the selected items.

1. la computadora portátil ¿Cuántas computadoras portátiles tienes?

 ____

2. el parlante inteligente ¿Qué escuchas en tu parlante inteligente?

 ____

3. el estéreo ¿Qué tipo de música te gusta?

 ____

4. los audífonos ¿Tienes audífonos para escuchar la música de tu servicio de distribución digital de música?

 ____

5. el DVD ¿Cuántos DVD tienes?

 ____

6. el servicio de distribución digital de música ¿Cuál es tu servicio de distribución de música favorito?

 ____

Nombre: ______________________________ Fecha: ______________

Repaso rápido: *Tener*

The verb *tener* (to have) is an irregular verb in the present tense. In addition to showing ownership, *tener* is used in various expressions where the verb **to be** is used in English. One such expression you already have learned is *tener* (+ number) *años*, which is used to talk about age.

yo	**tengo**	nosotros nosotras	**tenemos**
tú	**tienes**	vosotros vosotras	**tenéis**
Ud. él ella	**tiene**	Uds. ellos ellas	**tienen**

2 Use the information provided to form complete sentences, adding any necessary words.

MODELO: Ud. / tener / grabador de video digital
Ud. tiene un grabador de video digital.

1. tú / tener / consola de juegos

____

2. nosotros / tener / estéreo

____

3. Ud. / tener / computadora portátil

____

4. Alberto y Juan / tener / poco dinero

____

5. yo / tener / parlante inteligente

____

Nombre: ______________________________ Fecha: ______________

3 Combine items from each column to form complete sentences.

nosotros		una consola de juegos
tú		quince años
Uds.		un DVD
Marta	tener	un parlante inteligente
yo		mucho dinero
mi abuela		dos hermanas
mis amigos		un estéreo

1. ______________________________
2. ______________________________
3. ______________________________
4. ______________________________
5. ______________________________
6. ______________________________
7. ______________________________

4 Answer each question in a complete sentence.

1. ¿Cuántos años tienes?

   ____

2. ¿Cuántos hermanos tienes?

   ____

3. ¿Tiene tu familia un grabador de video digital?

   ____

4. ¿Qué DVD tienen tus amigos?

   ____

5. ¿Tiene el profesor/la profesora una computadora portátil en la clase de español?

   ____

6. ¿Tienen Uds. muchos o pocos exámenes en la clase de español?

   ____

Nombre: ______________________ Fecha: ______________

Repaso rápido: Expressing strong feelings with *¡Qué* (+noun)!

You have learned that the word *qué* can be combined with an adjective to form an exclamation, such as *¡Qué interesante!* It is also possible to combine the word *qué* with a noun to express strong feelings about a person, place or thing. For example, *¡Qué playa!* is the equivalent of **What a beach!**

5 Six exclamations are listed below. For each one, put the name of a person/place/thing that, in your opinion, merits such praise.

MODELO: ¡Qué ciudad! Barcelona

1. ¡Qué película! ______________________
2. ¡Qué actor! ______________________
3. ¡Qué ciudad! ______________________
4. ¡Qué música! ______________________
5. ¡Qué cantante! ______________________
6. ¡Qué restaurante! ______________________
7. ¡Qué profesor(a)! ______________________
8. ¡Qué carro! ______________________
9. ¡Qué tienda! ______________________
10. ¡Qué página web! ______________________

Nombre: ______________________________ Fecha: ______________

6 In this lesson you have learned about Costa Rica. Imagine that you are going to visit this Central American country in the near future. Use information from your textbook and other sources to say what you are going to do during your week in the land of the *ticos*.

MODELO: El lunes voy a ver San José.
El martes voy a ir al Parque Natural Monteverde.

Día	Actividades
el lunes	______________________________
	______________________________
el martes	______________________________
	______________________________
el miércoles	______________________________
	______________________________
el jueves	______________________________
	______________________________
el viernes	______________________________
	______________________________
el fin de semana (sábado y domingo)	______________________________
	______________________________

Nombre: ________________________________ Fecha: ______________

7 Imagine that you have the following plans and obligations in the next week. Rank them in order of what you most enjoy with number 1 being your favorite activity. Then compare your ranking with that of a classmate.

práctica de deportes ______

estudiar para un examen ______

montar en bicicleta ______

fiesta sorpresa ______

clase de piano ______

ir al cine ______

pasar tiempo con mi abuela ______

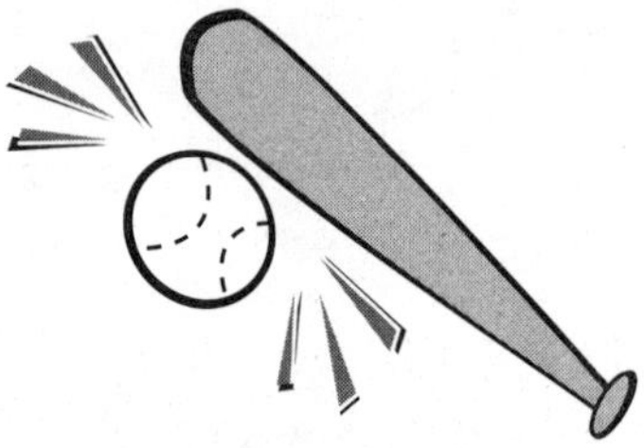

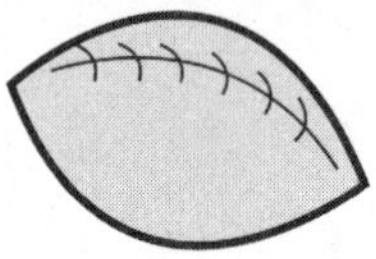

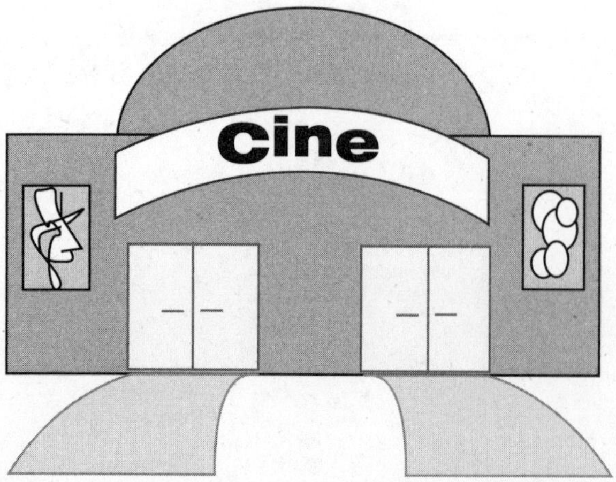

Nombre: ______________________________ Fecha: ______________

Repaso rápido: Direct object pronouns

A direct object in a sentence is the person or thing that receives the action of the verb and answers the question **what?** or **whom?**

They watch **the movie**.
We see **Arturo**.

A direct object pronoun can be used to replace a direct object that was previously mentioned (They watch **it**. We see **him**). The direct object pronouns (*los pronombres de complemento directo*) include:

me	*me*	**nos**	*us*
te	*you* (tú)	**os**	*you* (vosotros/as)
lo	*him, it, you* (Ud.)	**los**	*them, you* (Uds.)
la	*her, it, you* (Ud.)	**las**	*them, you* (Uds.)

The direct object pronouns *lo, la, los* and *las* can refer to people or objects. *Lo* can also refer to a nonspecific direct object, an idea or a phrase. To make a statement negative, place a negative word before the object pronoun.

In Spanish the word *a* precedes a direct object that refers to a person. For this reason it is called the *a personal*.

*Veo **a** Ana pero no veo **a** la profesora.*

At times the word *a* will be combined with the definite article *el* to form *al*.

*Veo **al** profesor pero no veo **a** los estudiantes.*

It is not necessary to use the *a personal* with the verb *tener*.

Andrés tiene seis primos.

Nombre: ______________________________ Fecha: ______________

8 Decide which of the following statements require the word *a* or *al*.

1. Vemos ______________ la profesora en la clase.
2. Comprendo ______________ el libro.
3. No me gusta ver ______________ los programas de televisión.
4. Voy a ver ______________ mis tíos el sábado.
5. Ella tiene ______________ una hermana.
6. Toco ______________ la guitarra.
7. Veo ______________ profesor de historia.

9 Change the following sentences, using direct object pronouns instead of stating the direct objects.

MODELO: Nosotros vemos a Carlos en la fiesta.
Nosotros lo vemos en la fiesta.

1. Ud. ve la película en el cine.

   ____

   ____

2. Tú ves los programas en casa.

   ____

   ____

3. Yo tengo la computadora portátil en la casa.

   ____

   ____

4. Ellos tienen el dinero en el banco.

   ____

   ____

Nombre: ______________________________ Fecha: ______________

10 The following questions ask about objects that you may see in your classroom. Answer each question in a complete sentence that includes a direct object pronoun.

1. ¿Ves el reloj?

____

2. ¿Ves la computadora?

____

3. ¿Ves el libro de español?

____

4. ¿Ven Uds. la ventana?

____

5. ¿Ven Uds. las revistas?

____

6. ¿Ven Uds. los mapas?

____

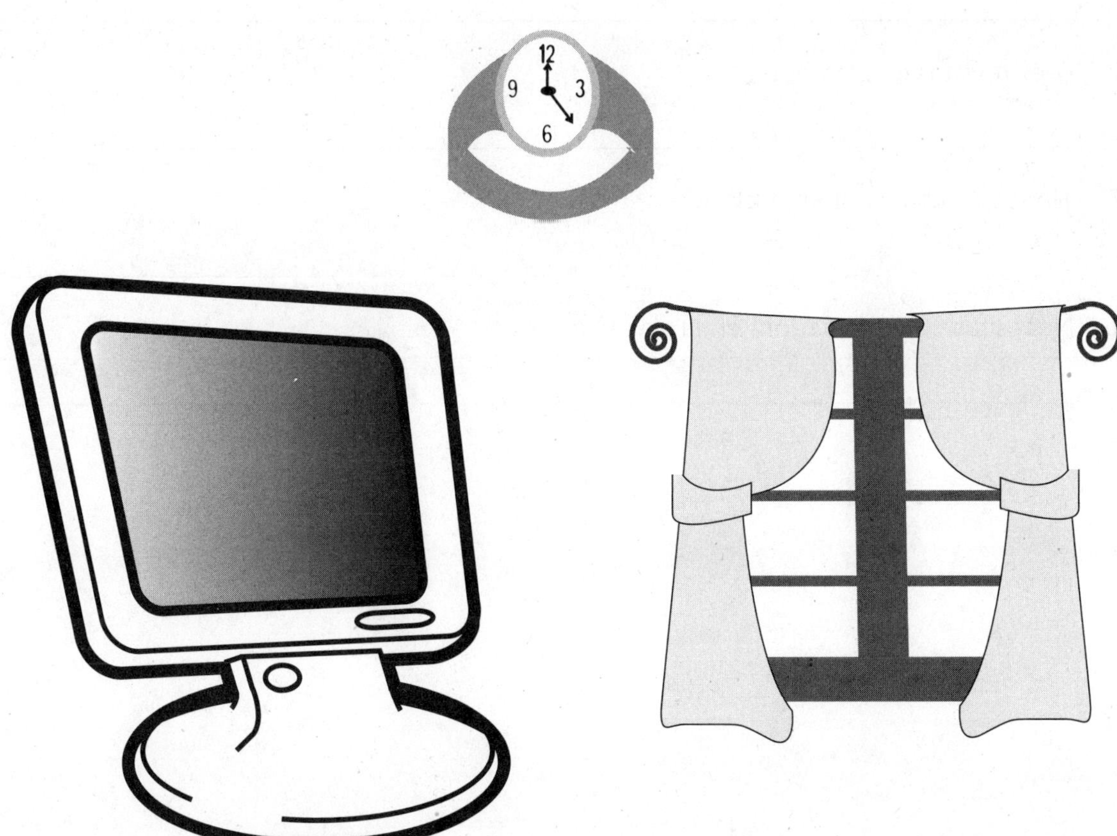

Nombre: ______________________________ Fecha: ______________

11 Answer the following questions about your Spanish class.

1. ¿Tienes amigos en la clase?

____

2. ¿Ves a tus amigos ahora?

____

3. ¿Comprendes al profesor o a la profesora de español?

____

4. ¿Comprendes el libro de español?

____

5. ¿Ves programas en la clase?

____

6. ¿Ves a los actores en los programas?

____

7. ¿Ves películas en la clase?

____

8. ¿Lees revistas en español?

____

9. ¿Tienes mucha tarea en la clase?

____

10. ¿Necesitas una calculadora en la clase?

____

Nombre: ______________________ Fecha: ______________

Lección B

1 Find six words related to the calendar that are spelled out in the grid.

E	L	G	G	Ó	T	F	S
M	A	Ñ	A	N	A	E	X
W	Y	N	H	I	Z	C	U
R	E	Q	O	V	O	H	Q
O	R	Í	Y	D	Í	A	O
A	N	T	E	A	Y	E	R
B	É	K	Z	Í	R	W	H

2 Answer the following questions in complete sentences.

1. ¿Qué día es hoy?

____

2. ¿Qué día es mañana?

____

3. ¿Qué día fue ayer?

____

4. ¿Qué día fue anteayer?

____

5. ¿Qué día es pasado mañana?

____

6. ¿Cuáles son los días del fin de semana?

____

7. ¿Cuál es tu día favorito? ¿Por qué te gusta?

____

Nombre: ______________________________ Fecha: ______________

Repaso rápido: *Venir*

In the preceding lesson you learned the verb *tener*. The conjugation of the irregular verb *venir* (to come) is very similar to the conjugation of *tener* in the present tense.

yo	**vengo**	nosotros nosotras	**venimos**
tú	**vienes**	vosotros vosotras	**venís**
Ud. él ella	**viene**	Uds. ellos ellas	**vienen**

3 Match the subject in the left column with the correct verb form in the right column.

1. ______ Ud.	A. vengo
2. ______ Manuel y Alvaro	B. venís
3. ______ yo	C. vienen
4. ______ nosotros	D. venimos
5. ______ tú	E. viene
6. ______ Patricia	F. vienes

4 Write sentences using the verb venir to say when different people are coming to a family reunion.

1. mis primos / 1:30

   ____

2. yo / 2:15

   ____

3. tú / 2:00

   ____

4. mi tía / 2:50

   ____

Nombre: ______________________________ Fecha: ______________

5 Imagine that you will soon celebrate your birthday with a party. Say who is coming to the party by completing the following paragraph with the correct forms of the verb *venir*.

Mañana es mi cumpleaños y vamos a tener una fiesta. Muchas personas (1)______________ a la fiesta. Por ejemplo, mi abuela (2)______________ en autobús y mis primos (3)______________ a pie. Mis padres y yo (4)______________ en carro del supermercado porque tenemos la comida y los refrescos.

Y tú, ¿(5)______________ a la fiesta?

6 Combine items from the three columns to say at what time different people come to school on a typical day.

nosotros		a las 6:45
Uds.		a las 7:00
mis amigos		a las 7:15
los profesores	venir	a las 7:30
tú		a las 7:45
yo		a las 8:00
el profesor/ la profesora de español		a las 8:15

1. ______________________________
2. ______________________________
3. ______________________________
4. ______________________________
5. ______________________________
6. ______________________________
7. ______________________________

Nombre: ______________________________ Fecha: ______________

Repaso rápido: Present tense to indicate the future

You have learned to express future plans with the pattern *ir* + *a* + infinitive. It is also possible to refer to the near future with the present tense of a verb as long as a future time expression is used or understood.

¿Tú vienes a la fiesta el viernes?	Are you coming to the party on Friday?
Sí, vengo a la fiesta.	Yes, I am coming to the party.
Mañana tengo seis clases.	Tomorrow I'll have six classes.

7 The following statements say what people are going to do in the next several days. Rewrite the statements to make them more immediate by using the present tense.

MODELO: Pilar va a tener una fiesta el sábado.
Pilar tiene una fiesta el sábado.

1. Yo voy a escribir un correo electrónico mañana.

____

2. Ud. va a comer con su familia el sábado.

____

3. Carolina va a ir al cine el jueves.

____

4. Mis amigas van a bailar el domingo.

____

5. Mis amigos y yo vamos a hablar el viernes.

____

6. Tú vas a venir a la fiesta de Pilar el sábado.

____

Nombre: ______________________________ Fecha: ______________

8 Match each month in the left column with an event in the right column.

1. ______ febrero
2. ______ julio
3. ______ noviembre
4. ______ marzo
5. ______ mayo
6. ______ enero
7. ______ junio

A. el Día de la Madre
B. el Día de San Patricio
C. el Día de Año Nuevo
D. el Día del Padre
E. el Día de San Valentín
F. el Día de Acción de Gracias
G. el Día de Independencia de EE.UU.

9 Make a list in which you identify your six favorite months. Then note why they are your favorites.

	Mes	**¿Por qué?**
1.	______________________	______________________
2.	______________________	______________________
3.	______________________	______________________
4.	______________________	______________________
5.	______________________	______________________
6.	______________________	______________________

10 Find six months that are spelled out in the grid.

O	M	U	S	I	D	O	J
C	A	B	R	I	L	J	U
T	Y	E	N	E	R	O	N
U	O	C	I	T	E	A	I
B	F	E	B	R	E	R	O
R	O	N	T	B	I	N	E
E	T	R	O	S	I	C	O

Nombre: ______________________________ Fecha: ______________

Repaso rápido: Using the numbers 101–999,999

Use *ciento* in place of *cien* for the numbers 101 to 199: *Tengo* ***cien*** *fotos en mi tableta y* ***ciento*** *veinte en mi teléfono celular.* The numbers from 200 to 999 have masculine and feminine forms that agree with the noun they describe: *Hay quinient****os*** *ochenta chic****os*** *y seiscient****as*** *cincuenta chic****as*** *en el colegio. Mil* (1,000) has only one form. Numbers beginning with *mil* are written with a period in Spanish instead of a comma: 1.000.

When the year is written in Spanish, it has no period. When it is spoken, it is read like any other four-digit number, **not** grouped two numbers at a time, as is done in English.

1926 = *mil novecientos veintiséis.*

11 Complete each addition problem. Remember that numbers beginning with *mil* are written with a period in Spanish instead of a comma.

MODELO: 2.000 + 5.500 = 7.500 siete mil quinientos

1. 6.300 + 3.200 = __________ ______________________________
2. 8.450 + 2.200 = __________ ______________________________
3. 50.000 + 25.000 = __________ ______________________________
4. 3.000 + 800.000 = __________ ______________________________
5. 200.000 + 750.000 = __________ ______________________________
6. 35.000 + 400.000 = __________ ______________________________

Nombre: ______________________ Fecha: ______________

Repaso rápido: Asking for and giving the date

Use the following pattern to give dates in Spanish: Form of *ser* + *el* + number for the day of month + *de* + month.

Es el 8 de julio.
Es el 21 de febrero.

Note: The word *primero* is used for the first day of the month instead of *uno*. The appropriate year may also be given by adding *de/del* to the pattern shown above.

Es el primero de marzo.
Es el veinticuatro de septiembre de mil novecientos noventa y nueve.
Es el ocho de octubre del dos mil.

12 For each item write the appropriate date in Spanish.

1. mi cumpleaños

____

2. la Navidad

____

3. el Día de San Patricio

____

4. el Día de Independencia de EE.UU.

____

5. el Día de Año Nuevo

____

6. hoy

____

Nombre: ______________________ Fecha: __________

13 In the left column write six events that your family celebrates each year. Then write the corresponding dates in the right column.

	Ocasión	Fecha
1.	______________	______________
2.	______________	______________
3.	______________	______________
4.	______________	______________
5.	______________	______________
6.	______________	______________

14 Write out the following years.

1. 711 ______________________________
2. 1492 ______________________________
3. 1789 ______________________________
4. 1814 ______________________________
5. 1898 ______________________________
6. 1939 ______________________________
7. 1975 ______________________________
8. 2006 ______________________________

Nombre: ______________________________ Fecha: ______________

Unidad 6

Lección A

1 The letters of the following kitchen items are in the wrong order. Put them in the correct order in order to spell each word correctly.

1. soav ______________________________
2. sopltavaal ______________________________
3. msae ______________________________
4. esfatu ______________________________
5. viastellres ______________________________
6. gaderfreo ______________________________
7. malpaár ______________________________
8. zlu ______________________________
9. dorargeirfre ______________________________

Nombre: ______________________ Fecha: __________

Repaso rápido: Expressing obligations with *tener que* and *deber*

The expressions *tener que* and *deber* are followed by an infinitive and have similar uses. *Tener que* states a need to do something while *deber* implies more of a moral obligation or what someone should do.

2 Use *tener que* to write a list of six things you and other family members have to do this week.

MODELO: Mi hermana tiene que estudiar para un examen.

1. ______________________
2. ______________________
3. ______________________
4. ______________________
5. ______________________
6. ______________________

3 Use *deber* to write a list of six things you and other family members should do this week.

MODELO: Yo debo hablar con mi abuelo.

1. ______________________
2. ______________________
3. ______________________
4. ______________________
5. ______________________
6. ______________________

Nombre: ______________________________ Fecha: ______________

Repaso rápido: Stem changing verbs *(e → ie)*

Some verbs require the spelling change *e* → *ie* in all forms of the present tense except for *nosotros* and *vosotros*. Such verbs include *pensar (ie), cerrar (ie), empezar (ie), encender (ie), preferir (ie), querer (ie)* and *sentir (ie).*

yo	p**ie**nso	nosotros nosotras	pensamos
tú	p**ie**nsas	vosotros vosotras	pensáis
Ud. él ella	p**ie**nsa	Uds. ellos ellas	p**ie**nsan

The verbs *tener* and *venir* also have this change except for the irregular *yo* forms (*tengo, vengo*).

¿Qué piensa Ud.?
¿Cuántos años tienes?
¿Viene Jaime a la fiesta?
Prefiero la bicicleta verde.
Ellos quieren comer a las dos.

The verb *pensar* has several uses when combined with other words.

When followed by an infinitive, *pensar* indicates what someone plans to do.

*Jorge **piensa ir** de compras.*

When combined with *en*, *pensar* indicates whom or what someone is thinking about.

¿En qué piensas?
Pienso en mi familia.

Pensar can be combined with *de* to ask for an opinion. In response to such a question, *pensar* is used with *que*.

¿Qué piensas de la clase de música?
Pienso que es excelente.

Nombre: ______________________________ Fecha: ______________

4 Choose a logical verb from the box and provide its correct form to complete each sentence.

cerrar	preferir	pensar	encender	empezar

1. Marisol ______________________________ la luz en la cocina.
2. Su madre ______________________________ la puerta de la casa.
3. Marisol y su madre ______________________________ a cocinar.
4. Su familia y yo ______________________________ comer a la una y media.
5. Yo ______________________________ comer arepas.

5 Combine items from the three columns to form logical sentences.

nosotros		ayudar en la cocina
Jorge	pensar	viajar a Venezuela
Luis y Ana	querer	poner la mesa
yo	preferir	comer poco
mis amigos y yo		comer mucho
tú		ayudar en la casa

1. ______________________________
2. ______________________________
3. ______________________________
4. ______________________________
5. ______________________________
6. ______________________________

Nombre: ______________________ Fecha: ______________

6 Friends are often very similar. Show this by rewriting the following statements as shown in the model.

MODELO: Prefiero estudiar en casa.
Preferimos estudiar en casa también.

1. Quiero ayudar en la cocina.

____

____

2. Pienso ver una película el sábado.

____

____

3. Empiezo a hacer la tarea a las siete.

____

____

4. Cierro la puerta de la cocina.

____

____

5. Enciendo la luz de la cocina.

____

____

6. Tengo que ayudar en la casa.

____

____

Nombre: ______________________ Fecha: ____________

7 Answer each question in a complete sentence.

1. ¿A qué hora empieza la escuela?

____

____

2. ¿A qué hora empieza la clase de español?

____

____

3. ¿Prefieres la clase de historia o la clase de matemáticas?

____

____

4. ¿Piensas estudiar el domingo?

____

____

5. ¿Dónde quieres vivir en el futuro?

____

____

6. ¿Qué quieres ser en el futuro?

____

____

Nombre: ______________________________ Fecha: ______________

8 Combine elements from the three columns to say what different people plan or intend to do next weekend.

yo		ayudar en la casa
tú		ir de compras
mi amiga		estudiar mucho
mi hermano	pensar	montar en bicicleta
mis amigos y yo		caminar en el parque
mis amigas		ir al centro
Uds.		tener una fiesta

1. ______________________________
2. ______________________________
3. ______________________________
4. ______________________________
5. ______________________________
6. ______________________________
7. ______________________________

9 Answer each question in a logical fashion.

1. ¿Qué piensas hacer el sábado?

   ____

2. ¿Qué piensas hacer el domingo?

   ____

3. ¿Dónde piensas vivir en el futuro?

   ____

4. ¿En qué o quién piensas mucho?

   ____

5. ¿Qué piensas de la clase de matemáticas?

   ____

Nombre: ______________________________ Fecha: ______________

10 Complete each sentence to say what items you have on the dinner table.

MODELO: Para la mantequilla tengo un cuchillo.

1. Para la sopa tengo ______________________________.
2. Para el agua tengo ______________________________.
3. Para el café tengo ______________________________.
4. Para la ensalada tengo ______________________________.
5. Para el pollo tengo ______________ y ______________.
6. La comida está en ______________________________.

11 Certain foods, beverages and events often go together. Match items from the two columns to show such combinations.

1. _____ la sal
2. _____ el pan
3. _____ el aceite
4. _____ el azúcar
5. _____ el postre
6. _____ la naranja

A. la mantequilla
B. el cumpleaños
C. la pimienta
D. el café
E. el vinagre
F. el jugo

12 Find six words that are spelled out in the grid.

I	P	O	V	M	E	C	A	T	E	L	I
U	O	P	I	M	T	A	Z	A	Q	U	E
P	S	J	N	U	Q	M	A	N	T	E	L
N	T	X	A	X	J	U	N	O	M	C	O
W	R	L	G	H	A	P	I	R	T	E	L
C	E	C	R	S	O	P	A	U	I	T	O
V	Y	E	E	L	I	N	T	E	S	A	L

Nombre: ______________________________ Fecha: ______________

Repaso rápido: Demonstrative adjectives

Demonstrative adjectives can be placed before a noun to indicate where someone or something is located in relation to yourself. Demonstrative adjectives must agree in gender and number with the nouns they modify.

singular		plural	
masculino	**femenino**	**masculino**	**femenino**
este	esta	estos	estas
ese	esa	esos	esas
aquel	aquella	aquellos	aquellas

To point out people or objects that are near to you, use *este*, *esta*, *estos* or *estas* (this/these).

Este postre es muy bueno.
Estos vasos son bonitos.

To refer to people or objects that are farther away, use *ese*, *esa*, *esos* or *esas* (that/those).

Esa cocina es muy grande.
Esas casas son nuevas.

To call attention to people or objects that are even farther away, use *aquel*, *aquella*, *aquellos* or *aquellas* (that/those over there).

Aquel restaurante es muy elegante.
Aquellas personas son de Caracas.

Nombre: ______________________________ Fecha: ______________

13 Fill in the blanks with the missing demonstrative adjectives and nouns.

	Singular	Plural
1.	esta lámpara	______________
2.	______________	aquellos chicos
3.	______________	esas tiendas
4.	aquella casa	______________
5.	______________	estos platos
6.	ese tenedor	______________
7.	este refrigerador	______________
8.	______________	esos vasos
9.	esa mesa	______________
10.	aquel restaurante	______________

14 You are planning a special dinner party for next Saturday at your home. Answer the following questions to help you get organized.

1. ¿Piensas tener mucha comida o poca comida?

   ____

2. ¿Prefieren tus amigos comer sopa o ensalada?

   ____

3. ¿Quieres tener un postre o dos postres diferentes?

   ____

4. ¿Qué tienes que comprar?

   ____

5. ¿A qué hora empieza la fiesta?

   ____

Nombre: ______________________________ Fecha: ______________

Lección B

1 Match the part of a house in the left column with an item in the right column.

1. ______ la cocina
2. ______ la sala
3. ______ el garaje
4. ______ el patio
5. ______ el comedor
6. ______ el baño

A. el carro
B. el televisor y el sofá
C. las plantas
D. la comida
E. el champú
F. el refrigerador

2 Complete the following sentences in a logical fashion in order to describe your home.

1. Mi casa está ______________________________.
2. Mi casa es ______________________________.
3. La cocina tiene ______________________________.
4. En la sala me gusta ______________________________.
5. El garaje tiene ______________________________.
6. En mi cuarto me gusta ______________________________.
7. En el comedor nosotros ______________________________.
8. En la piscina mis hermanos y yo ______________________________.
9. En la sala tengo ganas de ______________________________.
10. En el patio no me gusta ______________________________.

Nombre: ______________________________ Fecha: ______________

3 In the space below draw a floor plan of your home. Be sure to include and label each room.

4 Write seven statements about your home to accompany the drawing you completed in the previous activity.

1. ______________________________
2. ______________________________
3. ______________________________
4. ______________________________
5. ______________________________
6. ______________________________
7. ______________________________

Nombre: ______________________________ Fecha: ______________

Repaso rápido: *Decir*

The present tense of the verb *decir* has an irregular *yo* form and a stem change for all forms except *nosotros/as* and *vosotros/as*. *Decir* is used to report what is said.

yo	**digo**	nosotros nosotras	decimos
tú	dices	vosotros vosotras	decís
Ud. él ella	dice	Uds. ellos ellas	dicen

Manuel dice que el restaurante es muy bueno.
Ellos dicen que van a viajar a Colombia.

As shown in the preceding examples, it is necessary to put *que* after the verb *decir* when you summarize what someone says.

5 Use the information provided to form logical sentences.

1. Marisol / decir / Jorge / estar contento

____

2. yo / decir / la clase / ser interesante

____

3. nosotros / decir / la casa / ser bonito

____

4. tú / decir / la comida / ser bueno

____

5. Marisol y Jorge / decir / Cartagena / ser grande

____

Nombre: ______________________________ Fecha: ______________

Repaso rápido: Expressing wishes with *querer* or *gustaría*

To express wishes use either ***quiero* + infinitive** or the more polite ***me gustaría* + infinitive**.

Quiero ir a Venezuela.	I want to go to Venezuela.
Me gustaría ir a Venezuela.	I would like to go to Venezuela.

6 Complete each sentence in a logical fashion by writing four statements about yourself and four statements about a good friend.

1. Me gustaría viajar ______________________________.
2. Me gustaría tener ______________________________.
3. Quiero ir ______________________________.
4. Quiero comprar ______________________________.
5. Le gustaría viajar ______________________________.
6. Le gustaría tener ______________________________.
7. Quiere ir ______________________________.
8. Quiere comprar ______________________________.

7 Match the feeling in the left column with the action in the right column.

1. ______ tengo hambre	A. nado en la piscina
2. ______ tengo sed	B. tomo agua
3. ______ tengo prisa	C. como mucho
4. ______ tengo frío	D. corro a la escuela
5. ______ tengo ganas de caminar	E. voy al parque
6. ______ tengo calor	F. tomo chocolate caliente

Nombre: ______________________________ Fecha: ______________

8 Complete the crossword puzzle with the appropriate *tener* expressions.

Horizontales

2. quince
4. tomo un refresco
5. corro a mi casa
6. estoy en un accidente
7. debo

Verticales

1. en el verano hace 90 grados F.
3. quiero comer
4. estoy en mi cuarto por la noche

9 Complete each statement with the most logical *tener* expression.

1. A las 2:00 de la mañana yo ______________________________.
2. En el restaurante mis amigos ______________________________.
3. En una playa de Colombia nosotros ______________________________.
4. Durante una película de terror tú ______________________________.
5. Carolina corre mucho y no bebe agua. Ella ______________________________.

Nombre: ______________________________ Fecha: ______________

Repaso rápido: Regular present-tense verbs

You have studied many regular verbs and some verbs that have spelling changes or irregular forms. The present-tense endings for most verbs are summarized below.

cantar	**comprender**	**escribir**
cant**o**	comprend**o**	escrib**o**
cant**as**	comprend**es**	escrib**es**
cant**a**	comprend**e**	escrib**e**
cant**amos**	comprend**emos**	escrib**imos**
cant**áis**	comprend**éis**	escrib**ís**
cant**an**	comprend**en**	escrib**en**

10 Write a paragraph of seven to eight sentences about a typical day for you and your family. Be sure to include information about various relatives. You may create an imaginary family if you wish.

____

____

____

____

____

____

____

____

____

____

____

____

____

____

Nombre: ______________________________ Fecha: ______________

Repaso rápido: Stem-changing verbs (*e → i*)

Some verbs in Spanish require the spelling change *e → i* in all forms of the present tense except for *nosotros* and *vosotros*. Two examples are *pedir (i, i)* and *repetir (i, i)*. With the exception of its irregular *yo* form *(digo)*, the verb *decir* also follows this pattern.

yo	pido	nosotros nosotras	pedimos
tú	pides	vosotros vosotras	pedís
Ud. él ella	pide	Uds. ellos ellas	piden

Preguntar means "to ask a question," as does *hacer una pregunta*. *Pedir* means "to ask for, to request or to order (in a restaurant)." Other expressions with *pedir* include *pedir ayuda* (to ask for help), *pedir permiso* (to ask for permission), *pedir perdón* (to excuse oneself or ask forgiveness) and *pedir prestado/a* (to borrow).

11 Choose from the three verbs below and then write the correct form to complete each sentence.

pedir repetir **decir**

1. Mi padre ______________________ ayuda en la cocina.
2. Mi madre y mi padre ______________________ que vamos a comer a las seis.
3. Mi hermano habla mucho. Él ______________________ sus ideas.
4. En clase nosotros ______________________ las expresiones.
5. En el restaurante yo ______________________ un refresco.
6. No te gustan las mentiras. Tú siempre ______________________ la verdad.

Nombre: ______________________________ Fecha: ______________

12 Complete each sentence with the correct form of *pedir* or *preguntar*.

1. Juan siempre ____________________ ayuda a sus padres.
2. No sé dónde está la tienda. Por eso yo ____________________.
3. Luis y Ana ____________________ permiso para usar el carro de su abuelo.
4. Mi amigo no tiene reloj y siempre ____________________ qué hora es.
5. Cuando hay problemas, nosotros ____________________ perdón.
6. ¿Quién es ese chico? Voy a ____________________ cómo se llama.
7. Cuando hago la tarea de matemáticas, ____________________ prestada una calculadora.

13 Say what you do in each of the following situations.

1. No tengo dinero para ir al cine.

   ____

2. Digo una mentira muy mala.

   ____

3. Quiero usar el carro de mi hermana.

   ____

4. Tengo problemas en la clase de matemáticas.

   ____

5. No sé cuál es el número de teléfono de Pablo.

   ____

Nombre: ______________________ Fecha: ____________

Unidad 7

Lección A

1 Answer each question in a complete sentence.

1. ¿Cuáles son tus pasatiempos favoritos?

____

2. ¿Te gusta ver la televisión?

____

3. ¿Dónde hay televisores en tu casa?

____

4. ¿Te gustan las telenovelas?

____

5. ¿Qué programa te gusta mucho?

____

6. ¿A qué hora ves tu programa favorito?

____

7. En tu opinión, ¿quién es un actor muy bueno?

____

8. En tu opinión, ¿quién es una cantante excelente?

____

9. ¿Vas a ver la televisión esta noche? ¿Qué programa vas a ver?

____

____

10. ¿Haces las tareas antes de o después de ver la televisión?

____

Nombre: ______________________________ Fecha: ______________

2 Rank the following activities in your order of preference with number 1 being your favorite activity. Then write three statements with the verb *gustar* to summarize your likes and dislikes.

Actividad	**Clasificación**
1. jugar al ajedrez	_____
2. jugar a las damas	_____
3. jugar al básquetbol	_____
4. jugar al fútbol americano	_____
5. jugar a los videojuegos	_____
6. dibujar	_____
7. hacer aeróbicos	_____
8. leer el periódico	_____

MODELO: Me gusta mucho jugar al básquetbol.

1. ______________________________
2. ______________________________
3. ______________________________

3 Combine items from each column to form logical sentences.

a veces	yo	jugar a las cartas
muchas veces	tú	dibujar
una vez al día	mi amiga	jugar a los videojuegos
todos los días	mi abuela	leer el periódico
(casi) nunca	nosotros	hacer aeróbicos
(casi) siempre	mis amigos	jugar al ajedrez

1. ______________________________
2. ______________________________
3. ______________________________
4. ______________________________
5. ______________________________

Nombre: ______________________________ Fecha: ______________

Repaso rápido: Stem-changing verbs (*o* → *ue* and *u* → *ue*)

You already have learned that some verbs require a stem change (*e* → *ie* or *e* → *i*) in all forms of the present tense except *nosotros* and *vosotros*. Similarly, certain verbs have the change *o* → *ue* or *u* → *ue* in all present-tense forms except *nosotros* and *vosotros*. Two examples are *poder (ue)* and *jugar (ue)*.

poder		jugar	
p**ue**do	podemos	j**ue**go	jugamos
p**ue**des	podéis	j**ue**gas	jugáis
p**ue**de	p**ue**den	j**ue**ga	j**ue**gan

Yo juego al tenis y mi hermana juega al fútbol.
No puedo ir al partido el sábado.

Other verbs that require the *o* → *ue* stem change include *costar (ue)*, *recordar (ue)* and *volver (ue)*.

4 Choose the appropriate verb from the list and provide the correct form to complete each sentence.

jugar	poder	costar	recordar	volver

1. Nosotros ______________ al béisbol los sábados.
2. ¿______________ tú el número de teléfono de Rosa?
3. ¿Cuánto ______________ un televisor nuevo?
4. Mis amigos ______________ a casa a las cuatro.
5. María ______________ cantar muy bien.
6. Yo ______________ ir al partido.
7. Necesitamos estudiar más. Por eso nosotros ______________ a la biblioteca.
8. Los carros ______________ mucho dinero.
9. Tú ______________ muy bien al voleibol.
10. Carlos tiene dinero y por eso él ______________ ir de compras.

Nombre: ______________________ Fecha: ____________

5 Combine items from each column to form logical sentences.

nosotros		ir al partido
tú		ir a la fiesta
yo		salir esta noche
mis amigos	(no) poder	jugar al golf el sábado
Felipe		ver una película esta noche
Ud.		comprar una bicicleta nueva
Uds.		viajar a Argentina

1. ______________________
2. ______________________
3. ______________________
4. ______________________
5. ______________________
6. ______________________
7. ______________________

6 The members of José's family get home at different times in the afternoon/evening. Take the role of José to report when people return.

MODELO: Emilia / volver / las siete
Emilia vuelve a las siete.

1. Laura y yo / volver / las cinco

____

2. mi padre / volver / las seis

____

3. mis hermanas / volver / las cinco y media

____

4. yo / volver / las cinco

____

5. tú / volver / las ocho

____

Nombre: ______________________ Fecha: ____________

7 Connect the items in the left column with the numbers in the right column. Then write the appropriate unit of time next to each number, as shown in the model.

MODELO: hora ——— 60 minutos

1. semana — 100 ____________
2. año — 15 ____________
3. minuto — 31 ____________
4. siglo — 7 ____________
5. el mes de julio — 30 ____________
6. cuarto de hora — 24 ____________
7. media hora — 365 ____________
8. día — 60 ____________

8 Write sentences to explain your activities and plans in relation to each of the following time references.

MODELO: la semana que viene
La semana que viene voy a ir de compras.

1. hoy por la tarde

____

2. esta noche

____

3. mañana por la mañana

____

4. la semana que viene

____

5. en junio

____

Nombre: ______________________________ Fecha: ______________

Repaso rápido: Expressions with *hace*

Use the following pattern to describe an action that began in the past and continues in the present: *hace* + a time expression + *que* + the present tense of a verb.

Hace dos horas que estamos en casa.	We have been at home for two hours.
Hace tres años que Héctor estudia música.	Héctor has been studying music for three years.

The order of *hace* and the time expression is reversed to form a question beginning with *¿cuánto?*

¿Cuánto tiempo hace que estudias español?	How long have you been studying Spanish?
¿Cuánto tiempo hace que viven Uds. aquí?	How long have you lived here?

9 Tell how long the following activities have been taking place.

MODELO: yo / jugar al voleibol / dos años
Hace dos años que juego al voleibol.

1. nosotros / vivir aquí / cinco años

____

2. mi hermana / hacer aeróbicos / una hora

____

3. mis amigos / jugar al básquetbol / cuatro años

____

4. tú / estudiar biología / un año

____

5. Ud. / jugar al ajedrez / tres años

____

Nombre: ______________________________ Fecha: ______________

10 Answer the following questions to say how long you have done or had certain things.

1. ¿Cuánto tiempo hace que vives en esta ciudad?

____

____

2. ¿Cuánto tiempo hace que estudias en este colegio?

____

____

3. ¿Cuánto tiempo hace que estudias español?

____

____

4. ¿Cuánto tiempo hace que juegas tu deporte favorito?

____

____

5. ¿Cuánto tiempo hace que tienes un celular?

____

____

6. ¿Cuánto tiempo hace que tienes tu bicicleta?

____

____

7. ¿Cuánto tiempo hace que no ves televisión?

____

____

8. ¿Cuánto tiempo hace que no escuchas música?

____

____

Nombre: ______________________ Fecha: ______________

Repaso rápido: Present progressive

The *presente progresivo* is used to say what is happening right now. It is formed by combining the present tense of the verb *estar (estoy, estás, está, estamos, estáis, están)* with a present participle *(gerundio).*

Pilar está alquilando una película.	Pilar is renting a movie.
José y yo estamos viendo un partido.	José and I are watching a game.

To form the present participle of most verbs in Spanish, change the infinitive endings to *-ando* for an *-ar* verb or *-iendo* for an *-er* or *-ir* verb.

jug**ar**	→ jug**ando**	corr**er**	→	corr**iendo**	viv**ir**	→	viv**iendo**
cant**ar**	→ cant**ando**	pon**er**	→	pon**iendo**	cumpl**ir**	→	cumpl**iendo**
pens**ar**	→ pens**ando**	com**er**	→	com**iendo**	sal**ir**	→	sal**iendo**

Some *-ir* verbs that have a stem change in the present tense have a different stem change in the present participle. The second change is shown in parentheses after the infinitives.

verbo	**presente (yo)**	**gerundio**
dormir (ue, u)	duermo	durmiendo
preferir (ie, i)	prefiero	prefiriendo
sentir (ie, i)	siento	sintiendo
venir (ie, i)	vengo	viniendo

Note also the following spelling changes in the present participle:

pedir (i, i)	→	pidiendo	leer	→	leyendo
repetir (i, i)	→	repitiendo	poder	→	pudiendo

Nombre: ______________________ Fecha: ____________

11 Combine items from each column to say what different people are doing right now.

nosotros		ver la televisión
la profesora		jugar al fútbol
mis amigos		estudiar en el colegio
mi abuelo	estar	escribir en clase
yo		hablar por teléfono
tú		hacer aeróbicos
Ud.		tocar el piano

1. ______________________
2. ______________________
3. ______________________
4. ______________________
5. ______________________
6. ______________________
7. ______________________

12 Think of what you and others are typically doing at different times of the day. Look at the following people/hours and write complete sentences in the present progressive tense.

1. mis amigos y yo / 9:00 de la mañana

   ____

2. yo / 5:00 de la tarde

   ____

3. mi hermano/a / 10:30 de la noche

   ____

4. mis amigos / la medianoche

   ____

5. tú / 7:00 de la mañana

   ____

Nombre: ______________________ Fecha: ______________

13 Think of different people and what they are doing now. Write ten different names in the left column and then say what each person is doing in the right column.

	Nombre	Actividad
MODELO:	Clara	Clara está jugando a los videojuegos con sus amigos.
1.	______________	______________________________
2.	______________	______________________________
3.	______________	______________________________
4.	______________	______________________________
5.	______________	______________________________
6.	______________	______________________________
7.	______________	______________________________
8.	______________	______________________________
9.	______________	______________________________
10.	______________	______________________________

Nombre: ______________________________ Fecha: ______________

14 Use the cues to form complete statements about what different people are doing right now.

1. mi hermano / dormir en el sofá

   ____

2. Luis y Ana / escuchar la radio

   ____

3. yo / pensar en las vacaciones

   ____

4. tú / leer el periódico

   ____

5. nosotros / pedir / la comida

   ____

6. Uds. / repetir / la información

   ____

Nombre: ______________________________ Fecha: ______________

Repaso rápido: Using the present progressive with direct object pronouns

As you have learned, direct object pronouns usually precede conjugated verbs. However, direct object pronouns also may be attached to the end of an infinitive or to the end of a present participle.

La *voy a escribir.* *Voy a escribir**la**.*	I am going to write **it**. (the composition)
Lo *estamos viendo.* *Estamos viéndo**lo**.*	We are watching **it**. (the program)

Note that when a direct object pronoun is attached to a present participle, it is necessary to add an accent mark in order to maintain the original pronunciation of the present participle.

*Estoy comprándo**lo**.* I am buying **it**. (the book)

15 Answer each question affirmatively in two different ways.

MODELO: ¿Estás alquilando la película?
Sí, la estoy alquilando.
Sí, estoy alquilándola.

1. ¿Estás viendo la película?

____

____

2. ¿Estás comprando los refrescos?

____

____

3. ¿Estás leyendo el periódico?

____

____

4. ¿Están Uds. pidiendo la comida?

____

____

Nombre: ______________________________ Fecha: ______________

Lección B

1 Complete the crossword puzzle with words corresponding to seasons, weather and outdoor activities.

Horizontales

1. caminar
4. temperaturas altas
6. junio, julio y agosto
7. sobre ruedas o hielo

Verticales

1. marzo, abril y mayo
2. es de color amarillo
3. septiembre, octubre y noviembre
5. agua

Nombre: ______________________ Fecha: ____________

2 Answer each questions based on where you live.

1. ¿Qué tiempo hace en el verano?

____

2. ¿Qué tiempo hace en el invierno?

____

3. ¿Qué tiempo hace en la primavera?

____

4. ¿Qué tiempo hace en el otoño?

____

5. ¿Cuál es tu estación favorita? ¿Por qué te gusta?

____

____

6. ¿Qué te gusta hacer en el verano?

____

____

7. ¿Prefieres patinar o esquiar? ¿Por qué?

____

____

8. ¿Cuál es un lugar excelente en tu ciudad?

____

____

9. ¿En qué meses hace mucho sol?

____

____

10. ¿Qué estación del año no te gusta? ¿Por qué no?

____

____

Nombre: ______________________________ Fecha: ______________

Repaso rápido: Verbs that require special accentuation

You have learned that certain words in Spanish require a written accent mark. For example, some verbs that end in *-uar* or *-iar* require a written accent mark for all present-tense forms except *nosotros.* Such verbs include *esquiar, enviar* and *continuar* but not *copiar.*

yo esquío	*nosotros esquiamos*
yo envío	*nosotros enviamos*
yo continúo	*nosotros continuamos*

but:

yo copio	*nosotros copiamos*

3 Combine information from the three columns to write complete sentences. Pay special attention to verb forms that require written accents.

tú		una carta a Chile
mis amigos	esquiar	el número de teléfono
nosotros	enviar	en las montañas
yo	continuar	la competencia
Carlos	copiar	la información
Luisa y yo		un correo electrónico
Ud.		por la mañana

1. ____
2. ____
3. ____
4. ____
5. ____
6. ____
7. ____

Nombre: ______________________________ Fecha: ______________

Repaso rápido: Present tense of *dar* and *poner*

You have learned several verbs that are regular in the present tense except for their *yo* forms (*hago, sé, veo, salgo*). The verbs *dar* and *poner* also have irregular *yo* forms.

dar		poner	
doy	damos	**pongo**	ponemos
das	dais	pones	ponéis
da	dan	pone	ponen

Mis padres dan un paseo por la tarde.
Yo doy un paseo por la mañana.

Paco pone los platos en la cocina.
Yo pongo el pastel en la mesa.

4 Give the correct present-tense form of *poner* to complete each sentence.

1. Yo ______________________ la radio todos los días.
2. Mónica y Laura ______________________ la televisión para ver la telenovela.
3. Javier y yo ______________________ música salsa en las fiestas.
4. Don Roberto siempre ______________________ música clásica en el carro.
5. Margarita ______________________ la mesa todos los días para la comida.
6. Ramón y Arturo ______________________ los platos en el fregadero después de la comida.
7. ¿Qué música ______________________ tú cuando vas en carro?

Nombre: ______________________________ Fecha: ______________

5 There is a charity event at your school to help students in need. Write complete sentences to say what each person gives for charity, according to the cues. Follow the model.

MODELO: Pedro
<u>Pedro da tres reglas.</u>

1. Alberto

____

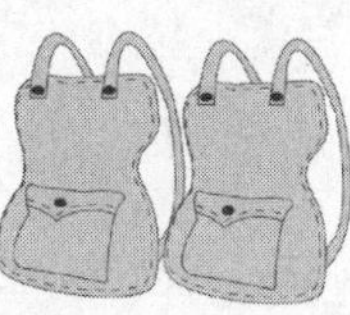

2. la profesora Martínez

____

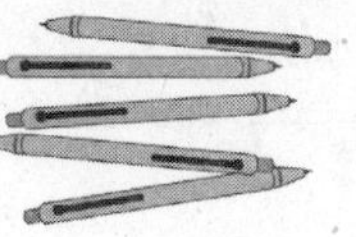

3. Maritza y yo

____

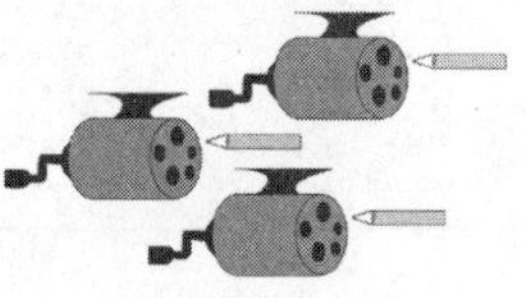

4. Rosa y Mario

____

5. Jorge y Alfredo

____

6. yo

____

7. tú

____

Nombre: ______________________________ Fecha: ______________

6 Find seven weather expressions in the grid.

P	F	O	P	Í	L	J	M	E	Á	Z	L
W	R	V	I	E	N	T	O	U	L	F	L
P	Í	U	C	E	Q	W	I	M	L	R	O
L	O	T	U	S	O	L	O	P	Í	E	V
N	E	V	A	R	U	T	I	P	O	S	E
G	R	I	M	I	L	É	T	I	H	C	R
L	T	É	B	P	M	A	N	A	P	O	D
L	T	E	M	P	E	R	A	T	U	R	A

7 Answer the questions to describe the weather where you live at different times of the year.

1. ¿Qué tiempo hace en abril?

____

2. ¿Qué tiempo hace en agosto?

____

3. ¿Qué tiempo hace en octubre?

____

4. ¿Qué tiempo hace en enero?

____

5. ¿En qué mes hace mal tiempo?

____

6. ¿En qué mes hace buen tiempo?

____

Nombre: ______________________ Fecha: __________

8 Write a paragraph of five to six sentences about your favorite season of the year. Be sure to include the following information: the name of the season, the typical weather, the outdoor activities you enjoy and why you prefer this season over the others.

9 For each weather condition listed, state an outdoor or indoor activity that you enjoy.

MODELO: Está nevando.
Me gusta esquiar.

1. Hace sol y calor.
2. Hace fresco y llueve.
3. Hace buen tiempo.
4. Hace viento y hace un poco de calor.
5. Hace mucho frío.

Nombre: ______________________________ Fecha: ______________

Repaso rápido: Describing people using *-dor* and *-ista*

You can identify someone who participates in a particular sport or activity by changing the ending on the sport to *-dor (-dora)* in some cases or *-ista* in others (which remains the same for males or females).

esquiar → el esquia**dor**/la esquia**dora**   el básquetbol → el/la basquetbol**ista**

Note: The accent mark is not used on the newly formed word when these endings are added.

10 The list below indicates several types of athletes. For each category put the name of a well-known athlete to match the sport/profession.

Nombre

1. tenista ______________________
2. beisbolista ______________________
3. ciclista ______________________
4. esquiador(a) ______________________
5. futbolista ______________________
6. basquetbolista ______________________
7. patinador(a) ______________________
8. corredor(a) ______________________

Nombre: ______________________________ Fecha: ______________

Repaso rápido: Using ordinal numbers

Los números ordinales (such as first, second and third) are used to place things in order. In Spanish only the first ten ordinal numbers are commonly used. They usually follow definite articles and precede nouns. Like other adjectives, the ordinal numbers must agree in gender and number with the nouns they modify.

El segundo día de la semana es martes.
Julio es el séptimo mes del año.

Elena fue la segunda nadadora en terminar.
Ana e Isabel fueron las primeras corredoras en terminar.

When *primero* and *tercero* precede a masculine singular noun, they are shortened to *primer* and *tercer*.

El primer día de la semana es lunes.
El tercer mes del año es marzo.

11 Answer the following questions about the calendar.

1. ¿Cuál es el primer mes del año?

   ____

2. ¿Cuál es el sexto mes del año?

   ____

3. ¿Cuál es el noveno mes del año?

   ____

4. ¿Cuál es el tercer día de la semana?

   ____

5. ¿Cuál es el quinto día de la semana?

   ____

Nombre: ______________________ Fecha: __________

12 In the left column make a list of your current classes. Then write statements to explain the order of the classes during the day.

MODELO: español — La primera clase es español.

1. ______________ ______________________
2. ______________ ______________________
3. ______________ ______________________
4. ______________ ______________________
5. ______________ ______________________
6. ______________ ______________________
7. ______________ ______________________

Nombre: ______________________________ Fecha: ______________

Unidad 8

Lección A

1 Match items from the two columns.

1. ______ arreglar
2. ______ cocinar
3. ______ comprar
4. ______ colgar
5. ______ hacer
6. ______ sacar

A. en el supermercado
B. la ropa
C. la casa
D. la cama
E. la basura
F. la paella

2 Combine items from the two columns to say how often you do the following things.

a veces
muchas veces
una vez al día
todos los días
(casi) siempre
(casi) nunca

sacar la basura
hacer la cama
cocinar para mi familia
colgar la ropa
arreglar la casa
comprar en el supermercado

MODELO: Todos los días hago la cama.

1. ______________________________
2. ______________________________
3. ______________________________
4. ______________________________
5. ______________________________
6. ______________________________

Nombre: ______________________________ Fecha: ______________

Repaso rápido: Direct object pronouns

You have learned that direct object pronouns show the person or thing in a sentence that receives the action of the verb. Direct object pronouns generally precede a conjugated verb but also can be attached to the end of an infinitive or to the end of a present participle.

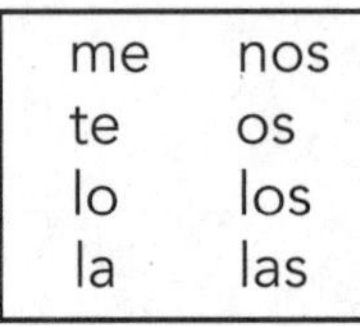

me	nos
te	os
lo	los
la	las

Limpio la casa. → *La limpio.*

Estoy limpiando la casa. → *La estoy limpiando.*
Estoy limpiándola.

Voy a limpiar la casa. → *La voy a limpiar.*
Voy a limpiarla.

3 Paula and her friends are doing different household chores. Rewrite each of the following statements using a direct object pronoun.

1. Miguel y Rosa están comprando la comida.

   ____

2. Javier está cocinando la paella.

   ____

3. Nosotros estamos limpiando la casa.

   ____

4. Estoy arreglando la sala.

   ____

5. Ana está adornando el patio.

   ____

Nombre: ______________________________ Fecha: ______________

Repaso rápido: Indirect object pronouns

The indirect object is the person in a sentence **to whom** or **for whom** something is said or done.

I am talking **to you**. We are going to buy a present **for him**.

An indirect object pronoun (*pronombre de complemento indirecto*) is sometimes used in place of an indirect object. You already have used the indirect object pronouns with the verb *gustar*. They look the same as the direct object pronouns with the exception of *le* and *les*.

me	*to me, for me*	**nos**	*to us, for us*
te	*to you, for you*	**os**	*to you, for you* (vosotros/as)
le	*to you, for you* (Ud.) *to him, for him* *to her, for her*	**les**	*to you, for you* (Uds.) *to them, for them*

The rules for placement of indirect object pronouns are the same as those you learned for direct object pronouns.

They usually precede a conjugated verb but may be attached to an infinitive or a present participle. In the case of the present participle, you have to add an accent mark to maintain the original pronunciation.

Te *voy a decir un secreto.* *Voy a decir**te** un secreto.*	I am going to tell **you** a secret.
*Ana **me** está hablando.* *Ana está hablándo**me**.*	Ana is talking **to me**.

Place any negative expressions before the indirect object pronouns.

No les *voy a escribir hoy.*	I'm **not** going to write **to them** today.
Nunca nos *dicen la verdad.*	They **never** tell **us** the truth.

When you use the indirect object pronoun *le* it may be necessary to add *a Ud., a él, a ella* or *a* + noun for clarity or emphasis. Similarly, the indirect object pronoun *les* may be accompanied by *a Uds., a ellos, a ellas* or *a* + plural noun.

Le doy la receta a Ud. *Les doy la receta a Uds.*

Nombre: ______________________________ Fecha: ______________

4 Imagine that different people are helping you today because you are in a hurry. Say what the following friends and relatives are doing for you.

MODELO: Marta / preparar la comida
<u>Marta me está preparando la comida. / Marta está preparándome la comida.</u>

1. mi hermano / hacer la cama

   ____

2. mi madre / arreglar la sala

   ____

3. Carlos / limpiar el cuarto

   ____

4. mis abuelos / comprar la comida

   ____

5. mi padre / lavar la ropa

   ____

5 Imagine that different people are exchanging gifts in a family celebration. Combine items from each column to say who is giving what to whom.

yo	me		un reloj
tú	te		un libro
mi hermana	le	dar	una computadora portátil
nosotros	nos		un videojuego
mis padres	les		una camiseta

MODELO: <u>Yo te doy un libro.</u>

1. ______________________________
2. ______________________________
3. ______________________________
4. ______________________________
5. ______________________________

Nombre: ______________________________ Fecha: ______________

6 Answer each question in a complete sentence. In the first four answers you will identify people who do something to you or for you. In the last four answers you will indicate whether you do the same things in return.

1. ¿Quién te escribe cartas por correo electrónico?

   ____

2. ¿Quién te habla por teléfono?

   ____

3. ¿Quiénes te preparan la comida?

   ____

4. ¿Quiénes te compran la comida?

   ____

5. ¿Le escribes cartas por correo electrónico también?

   ____

6. ¿Le hablas por teléfono también?

   ____

7. ¿Les preparas la comida también?

   ____

8. ¿Les compras la comida también?

   ____

Nombre: ________________________________ Fecha: ______________

7 Combine items from each column to summarize the e-mail correspondence of your family and friends.

yo			a mis amigos
mis amigos			a mi hermano
nosotros	le		a mi tío
mi hermana	les	escribir	a mis abuelos
mis primos			a mis primos
mi madre			a mi hermana
mi padre			a mi prima
mis tías			a mis profesores

MODELO: Mi hermana les escribe a mis primos.

1. ______________________________
2. ______________________________
3. ______________________________
4. ______________________________
5. ______________________________
6. ______________________________
7. ______________________________
8. ______________________________

Nombre: ______________________________ Fecha: ______________

Repaso rápido: Saying what just happened with *acabar de*

You can express what has just happened in the recent past by using a form of the verb *acabar* followed by *de* and an infinitive.

Rosa acaba de ir al supermercado.	Rosa has just gone to the supermarket.
Acabamos de limpiar la casa.	We have just cleaned the house.

8 Imagine that you and your family have just finished doing household chores. Combine items from each column to say the tasks that different people have completed.

nosotros		colgar la ropa
mi hermana		comprar la comida
mi padre	acabar de	cocinar
mis abuelos		limpiar la sala
yo		arreglar el cuarto
mis hermanos		sacar la basura

MODELO: Yo acabo de colgar la ropa.

1. ______________________________
2. ______________________________
3. ______________________________
4. ______________________________
5. ______________________________
6. ______________________________

Nombre: ______________________ Fecha: ____________

9 Complete the crossword puzzle with words pertaining to household chores.

1
2 3 4
5
6 7
8
9

Horizontales

3. la comida
5. la mesa
6. ir a la tienda para
8. los platos sucios
9. el cuarto

Verticales

1. sacar
2. pasar
4. después de comer
6. el piso
7. la ropa limpia en el cuarto

Nombre: ______________________________ Fecha: ______________

10 Some household chores are more pleasant than others. Rank the following tasks in your order of preference and then write five statements with *tener que* to summarize the things you have to do on a regular basis.

Los quehaceres	**Mis preferencias**
1. colgar la ropa	________
2. arreglar mi cuarto	________
3. poner la mesa	________
4. dirigir el trabajo	________
5. ir a buscar leche/pan	________
6. lavar los platos	________
7. sacar la basura	________
8. recoger la mesa	________
9. pasar la aspiradora	________
10. preparar la comida	________

MODELO: Tengo que ir a buscar leche.

1. ______________________________
2. ______________________________
3. ______________________________
4. ______________________________
5. ______________________________

Nombre: ______________________ Fecha: ____________

Repaso rápido: Present tense of *oír* and *traer*

The verbs *oír* and *traer* are irregular in the present tense.

oír		**traer**	
oigo	oímos	traigo	traemos
oyes	oís	traes	traéis
oye	oyen	trae	traen

gerundio: oyendo

gerundio: trayendo

11 Form complete sentences to say what the following people hear on the radio.

MODELO: Uds. / música popular
Uds. oyen música popular.

1. mi padre / música clásica
____

2. yo / música popular
____

3. nosotros / las noticias
____

4. tú / música salsa
____

5. mis abuelos / un programa nuevo
____

Nombre: ______________________ Fecha: ____________

12 Combine items from each column to say what different people are bringing to a picnic.

nosotros		la música
mi abuela		los platos
Susana		el postre
yo	traer	la comida
Uds.		los vasos
Javier		el estéreo
tú		los refrescos
Clara y Rosa		las servilletas
mis tíos		los cubiertos

MODELO: Mi abuela trae el postre.

1. ______________________
2. ______________________
3. ______________________
4. ______________________
5. ______________________
6. ______________________
7. ______________________
8. ______________________

Nombre: ______________________________ Fecha: ______________

Repaso rápido: Preterite tense of *-ar* verbs

The preterite tense is used to discuss actions or events that were completed in the past. To form the preterite tense of regular *-ar* verbs, remove the *-ar* ending from the infinitive and add the endings shown below.

trabajar

yo	trabaj**é**	nosotros nosotras	trabaj**amos**
tú	trabaj**aste**	vosotros vosotras	trabaj**asteis**
Ud. él ella	trabaj**ó**	Uds. ellos ellas	trabaj**aron**

Regular verbs that end in *-car, -gar* and *-zar* have a spelling change in the *yo* form of the preterite tense in order to maintain the original pronunciation of the infinitive.

bus**car** → bus**qué** apa**gar** → apa**gué** empe**zar** → empe**cé**

13 Choose from the following verbs to say what different people did yesterday. Add additional information to form complete sentences.

comprar estudiar trabajar lavar cocinar tocar

MODELO: tú <u>Tú tocaste el piano.</u>

1. yo ______________________________
2. mi amiga ______________________________
3. mis amigos ______________________________
4. el/la profesor(a) ______________________________
5. mis amigos y yo ______________________________
6. tú ______________________________

Nombre: ______________________________ Fecha: ______________

Lección B

1 Match each food in the left column with its most typical color in the right column. You will use some colors more than once.

1. ______ el tomate
2. ______ el guisante
3. ______ el arroz
4. ______ el aguacate
5. ______ la banana
6. ______ el ajo
7. ______ la lechuga

A. blanco
B. verde
C. amarillo
D. rojo
E. azul
F. negro
G. gris

2 You are going to prepare a dinner of *ensalada* and *paella*. Write a shopping list of the things you will need to buy.

Para la ensalada	Para la paella
______________________	______________________
______________________	______________________
______________________	______________________
______________________	______________________
______________________	______________________
______________________	______________________
______________________	______________________
______________________	______________________

Nombre: ______________________ Fecha: ____________

3 Answer the following questions in complete sentences.

1. ¿Te gusta cocinar?

   ____

2. En tu familia, ¿a quién le gusta mucho cocinar?

   ____

3. ¿Qué comida te gusta preparar?

   ____

4. ¿Tienes una receta favorita? ¿Cuál es?

   ____

5. ¿Qué compras en el supermercado?

   ____

6. ¿Prefieres comprar en un supermercado o un mercado? ¿Por qué?

   ____

7. ¿Cuál es tu comida favorita?

   ____

8. ¿Qué comida no te gusta?

   ____

9. ¿Te gustan las verduras? ¿Cuál es tu favorita?

   ____

Nombre: ______________________________ Fecha: ______________

4 Form complete sentences with the information provided.

MODELO: a mí / importar / comer bien
<u>(A mí) me importa comer bien.</u>

1. a nosotros / hacer falta / el arroz
____

2. a Teresa / parecer bien / comer una paella
____

3. a mí / importar / los precios en el supermercado
____

4. a ti / hacer falta / los refrescos para la fiesta
____

5. a Uds. / parecer mal / no tomar leche
____

6. a Clara / importar / el pastel
____

5 Combine items from each column to form complete sentences.

a mí			ir al mercado
a ti	me		importante comer bien
a Ud.	te	hacer falta	comprar el queso
a mi hermana	le	parecer	saber los precios
a nosotros	nos	importar	cocinar esta noche
a Uds.	les		ir al supermercado
a mis padres			tener comida fresca

1. ______________________________
2. ______________________________
3. ______________________________
4. ______________________________
5. ______________________________
6. ______________________________
7. ______________________________

Nombre: ______________________________ Fecha: ______________

Repaso rápido: Making comparisons

Comparisons are used to compare people or things. Follow these patterns:

más/menos + adjective/adverb + *que*	*tan* + adjective/adverb + *como*
más/menos + noun + *que*	*tanto,-a,-os,-as* + noun + *como*
verb + *más/menos que*	verb + *tanto como*

Some adjectives and adverbs have irregular comparative forms: *bueno,-a (mejor), bien (mejor), malo,-a (peor), mal (peor), grande (mayor/más grande), pequeño,-a (menor/más pequeño,-a), joven (menor/más joven), viejo,-a (mayor/más viejo,-a).*

When making comparisons it is also common to single out a person, group, object or attribute as the best, worst, most or least. Such statements are called superlatives and use the following patterns:

definite article (+ noun) + *más/menos* + adjective (or an irregular comparative)

*La paella es **la comida más popular**.* Paella is **the most popular food**.

verb + *lo* + *más/menos* + adverb + *posible*

*Debes ir a la tienda **lo más pronto** posible.* You should go to the store **as soon as** possible.

6 Write complete sentences to express logical comparisons of the items given.

MODELO: la comida fresca / la comida en lata
La comida fresca es más natural que la comida en lata.

1. los supermercados / los mercados

____

2. la comida mexicana / la comida española

____

3. los restaurantes / las cafeterías

____

4. la carne / el pollo

____

Nombre: ______________________________ Fecha: ______________

7 Write complete sentences to express logical comparisons of the items given.

MODELO: la clase de español / la clase de biología
La clase de español es más interesante que la clase de biología.

1. la televisión / el cine

____

2. el tenis / el básquetbol

____

3. el béisbol / el fútbol

____

4. la música rock / la música clásica

____

5. el verano / el invierno

____

8 The following six statements tell you some things about Manuel. After each statement write a sentence in which you compare yourself to him.

MODELO: Manuel tiene tres hermanas.
Yo tengo tantas hermanas como él.

1. Manuel tiene un hermano.

____

2. Manuel tiene diez primos.

____

3. Manuel tiene veinte años.

____

4. Manuel tiene una computadora portátil.

____

5. Manuel toca tres instrumentos musicales.

____

6. Manuel cocina todos los días.

____

Nombre: ______________________________ Fecha: ______________

9 Write complete sentences to identify the following places in the city where you live.

MODELO: el parque más popular
El parque más popular de mi ciudad es el Parque Nacional.

1. el supermercado más grande

____

2. el peor restaurante

____

3. los mejores restaurantes

____

4. la tienda más elegante

____

5. el lugar más bonito

____

10 Imagine that your family is preparing for a party. Say what different people are doing, according to the following cues.

MODELO: yo / limpiar / bien
Yo limpio lo mejor posible.

1. nosotros / arreglar la sala / pronto

____

2. mi padre / cocinar / temprano

____

3. mis hermanos / barrer el suelo / bien

____

4. yo / comprar el pastel / rápidamente

____

5. mi madre / poner la mesa / pronto

____

Nombre: ______________________________ Fecha: ______________

11 Complete the crossword puzzle with the appropriate food vocabulary.

Horizontales

1. carne típica en la paella
2. no la comen los vegetarianos
3. verdura para la ensalada
6. postre típico bien frío
7. verdura de color verde, rojo o amarillo
11. fruta popular en pasteles
12. fruta pequeña y roja

Verticales

1. comida típica de España
4. postre muy dulce
5. verdura verde y pequeña
8. cereal de color amarillo
9. tipo de carne
10. bebida caliente popular por la mañana

Nombre: ______________________ Fecha: ______________

12 Develop a menu for breakfast, lunch and dinner at your home. Be sure to have a balanced diet and do not include any item more than once.

Menú

el desayuno	el almuerzo	la cena
____________	____________	____________
____________	____________	____________
____________	____________	____________
____________	____________	____________
____________	____________	____________

de tomar:

____________	____________	____________

Nombre: ______________________________ Fecha: ______________

13 Answer each question to describe your food preferences.

1. ¿Comes muchas o pocas frutas?

____

2. ¿Cuál es tu fruta favorita?

____

3. ¿Comes muchas o pocas verduras?

____

4. ¿Cuál es tu verdura preferida?

____

5. ¿Prefieres comer carne o pescado?

____

6. ¿Qué helados te gustan?

____

7. ¿Qué comida te gusta preparar?

____

8. ¿Prefieres comprar en un mercado o en un supermercado? ¿Por qué?

____

Nombre: ______________________________ Fecha: ______________

Repaso rápido: More about the preterite

You already have learned the preterite tense endings of regular *-ar* verbs.

cocinar

yo	cocin**é**	nosotros nosotras	cocin**amos**
tú	cocin**aste**	vosotros vosotras	cocin**asteis**
Ud. él ella	cocin**ó**	Uds. ellos ellas	cocin**aron**

Unlike regular *-ar* verbs such as *cocinar*, the verbs *dar* and *estar* are irregular in the preterite tense.

dar		**estar**	
di	dimos	estuve	estuvimos
diste	disteis	estuviste	estuvisteis
dio	dieron	estuvo	estuvieron

14 Choose from the infinitives in the box and provide the correct preterite-tense verb forms to complete the paragraph.

estar dar tomar hablar preparar

El sábado pasado mis padres (1) ______________ una fiesta para celebrar el cumpleaños de mi abuela. Todos mis tíos y primos (2) ______________ en la fiesta y mi sobrina también (3) ______________. Nosotros (4) ______________ mucho con la abuela. Mi madre (5) ______________ una paella deliciosa para la fiesta. Yo le (6) ______________ chocolates a mi abuela y mi hermana le (7) ______________ un libro. Mi abuela (8) ______________ muy contenta con la comida y los regalos.

Nombre: ______________________________ Fecha: ______________

15 Combine items from each column to say where different people were last Friday evening.

Alejandro		la fiesta de cumpleaños de Ana
David y yo		el cine
mis amigos	estar en	el partido de fútbol
tú		el concierto de rock
yo		el supermercado
Ud.		el teatro

1. ______________________________
2. ______________________________
3. ______________________________
4. ______________________________
5. ______________________________
6. ______________________________

Nombre: ______________________________ Fecha: ______________

Unidad 9

Lección A

1 Say what clothing you typically wear to the following locations and events.

1. la playa ______________________________
2. el colegio ______________________________
3. una fiesta forma ______________________________
4. una fiesta informal ______________________________
5. un partido de fútbol americano ______________________________
6. un baile del colegio ______________________________
7. un concierto ______________________________

2 Match the item in the left column with the body part in the right column.

1. ______	los calcetines	A. el dedo
2. ______	el sombrero *(hat)*	B. las manos
3. ______	la ropa	C. las piernas
4. ______	los guantes *(gloves)*	D. los pies
5. ______	el pantalón	E. la cabeza
6. ______	el anillo *(ring)*	F. los brazos
7. ______	la camisa	G. el cuerpo

Nombre: ______________________ Fecha: ____________

3 Answer the following questions in complete sentences.

1. ¿Qué ropa llevas hoy?

____

2. ¿Cuál es tu color favorito para la ropa?

____

3. ¿Quién lleva traje y corbata al colegio?

____

4. ¿En qué estación del año necesitas un suéter?

____

5. ¿Qué ropa necesitas para esquiar en las montañas?

____

4 Combine items from the two columns to describe some of the clothing that you own.

La ropa	Los colores
la camisa	anaranjado
el pantalón	amarillo
los zapatos	rosado
el traje	verde
el vestido	marrón
la blusa	negro
la falda	morado

MODELO: Tengo una camisa roja.

1. ______________________
2. ______________________
3. ______________________
4. ______________________
5. ______________________

Nombre: ______________________ Fecha: ____________

Repaso rápido: Adjectives as nouns

Remember that a definite article is required when naming colors in Spanish because they are considered nouns.

Prefiero ***el*** *(color) azul.*	I prefer blue.

In addition, sometimes a word being described may be omitted in order to avoid repeating a noun. In such cases the article remains and the adjective must agree with the noun that was omitted.

¿Te gusta la camisa blanca o ***la*** *(camisa)* ***azul****?*	Do you like the white shirt or **the blue one**?

5 Say how many of the following items you have and give a description of them.

MODELO: camisa — Tengo dos camisas, una roja y una blanca.

1. zapatos ______________________
2. botas ______________________
3. traje de baño ______________________
4. pijama ______________________
5. medias / calcetines ______________________
6. *jeans* ______________________

Nombre: ______________________________ Fecha: ______________

Repaso rápido: Preterite of *-er* and *-ir* verbs

Remove the last two letters from the infinitive and add the appropriate endings.

correr		vivir	
corrí	corr**imos**	viví	viv**imos**
corr**iste**	corr**isteis**	viv**iste**	viv**isteis**
corr**ió**	corr**ieron**	viv**ió**	viv**ieron**

The *-ir* verbs that have a stem change in the present tense also require a stem change in the preterite tense: *dormir (ue,* ***u****), sentir (ie,* ***i****), pedir (i,* ***i****), preferir (ie,* ***i****), mentir (ie,* ***i****), repetir (i,* ***i****)*. This second change only occurs for *Ud., él, ella, Uds., ellos* and *ellas*.

dormir		sentir		pedir	
dormí	dormimos	sentí	sentimos	pedí	pedimos
dormiste	dormisteis	sentiste	sentisteis	pediste	pedisteis
d**u**rmió	d**u**rmieron	s**i**ntió	s**i**ntieron	p**i**dió	p**i**dieron

6 Use the information provided to say what different people did yesterday.

1. nosotros / comer en un restaurante

   ____

2. mi amiga / pedir una ensalada

   ____

3. Uds. / escribir una carta

   ____

4. yo / aprender mucho en mi clase de español

   ____

5. Ud. / dormir muchas horas

   ____

6. tú / correr / tres kilómetros

   ____

Nombre: ____________________ Fecha: __________

7 Combine items from each column to form seven logical statements about last weekend.

mis amigos	trabajar	en la tienda de ropa
yo	dormir	en el centro comercial
nosotros	comprar	en una fiesta
Ud.	pedir	pocas horas
mi amiga	escribir	una chaqueta
tú	estar	mucha fruta
mis primos	comer	una composición

1. ____________________
2. ____________________
3. ____________________
4. ____________________
5. ____________________
6. ____________________
7. ____________________

8 Choose from the infinitives listed below and provide the correct preterite-tense verb forms to complete the paragraph.

comprar	estar	tomar	pedir	comer

El sábado pasado mi amiga y yo (1) ____________ en el centro comercial. Después de mirar en muchas tiendas yo (2) ____________ un abrigo negro y mi amiga (3) ____________ una chaqueta azul. Luego nosotros (4) ____________ en un restaurante excelente. Mi amiga (5) ____________ carne con papas y yo (6) ____________ un sandwich de pollo. Para terminar el día nosotros (7) ____________ en el cine del centro comercial para ver una película. Otras amigas también (8) ____________ en el cine y después de la película nosotros (9) ____________ un refresco con ellas. ¡Fue un día muy bueno!

Nombre: ______________________________ Fecha: ______________

9 Complete the following crossword puzzle.

Horizontales

1. Este __ amarillo me gusta mucho.
2. ¿No le gusta __ de estos pantalones?
4. Esta camisa la puedo __ con mi corbata nueva.
6. Tengo un solo __. No sé dónde está el otro.
8. ¿Tienen un __ de lana?
9. Prefiero llevar esta __ y no aquel impermeable.
10. ¿Tienen abrigos rojos? No, no nos queda __.

Verticales

1. El __ se lleva en la cabeza.
3. Esta chaqueta me __ muy grande.
4. Ayer fui al centro __ Plaza Paitilla.
5. No me gusta __ de estas chaquetas.
7. ¿Hay __ a quién preguntar?

Nombre: ______________________ Fecha: ______________

Repaso rápido: Preterite tense of *ir* and *ser*

The irregular preterite tense forms of the verbs *ir* and *ser* are identical.

ir/ser	
fui	fuimos
fuiste	fuisteis
fue	fueron

*¿**Fuiste** al partido ayer?*	**Did you go** to the game yesterday?
*Sí, **fui** al partido y **fue** bueno.*	Yes, **I went** to the game and **it was** good.

10 Write complete sentences to say where different people went last weekend.

MODELO: mi amigo / ir / el parque
Mi amigo fue al parque.

1. nosotros / ir / el centro comercial

   ____

2. mis tíos / ir / el teatro

   ____

3. yo / ir / el parque

   ____

4. Teresa / ir / el supermercado

   ____

5. tú / ir / el cine

   ____

6. Ud. / ir / el centro

   ____

Nombre: ______________________________ Fecha: ______________

11 In the preceding exercise you wrote six statements about where people went last weekend. Now write logical statements to say what they did while they were at those locations.

MODELO: Mi amigo fue al parque.
Él corrió y caminó en el parque.

1. ______________________________
2. ______________________________
3. ______________________________
4. ______________________________
5. ______________________________
6. ______________________________

12 Write a paragraph of seven to eight sentences about last weekend. Be sure to explain where you and other people went and what you did.

____
____
____
____
____
____
____

Nombre: ______________________________________ Fecha: ______________

Repaso rápido: Affirmative and negative words

The following chart shows common affirmative and negative expressions.

sí *(yes)*	**no** *(no)*
algo *(something, anything)*	**nada** *(nothing, anything)*
alguien *(somebody, anybody)*	**nadie** *(nobody, anybody)*
algún, alguna,-os,-as *(some, any)*	**ningún, ninguna,-os,-as** *(none, not any)*
o...o *(either...or)*	**ni...ni** *(neither...nor)*
siempre *(always)*	**nunca** *(never)*
también *(also, too)*	**tampoco** *(neither, either)*

In Spanish it is possible to put a negative expression before the verb and one or more negative expressions after the verb. It is also common for certain negative expressions to be used alone before the verb.

Luis ***no*** *entra* ***nunca*** *en aquella tienda.*
Luis **never** enters that store.
Luis ***nunca*** *entra en aquella tienda.*

When *nadie* or a form of *ninguno* are direct objects referring to people, the personal *a* is required.

No *veo* ***a nadie*** *en la oficina.*	I don't see anyone in the office.
No *veo* ***a ninguna*** *amiga aquí.*	I don't see any friend here.

13 Match the affirmative expression in the left column with its opposite negative expression in the right column.

1. ______ alguien
2. ______ siempre
3. ______ algo
4. ______ también
5. ______ alguna
6. ______ o...o

A. nada
B. tampoco
C. ni...ni
D. nadie
E. nunca
F. ninguna

Nombre: ______________________________ Fecha: ______________

14 Make the affirmative statements negative and the negative statements affirmative.

1. Siempre compramos en esa tienda.

   ____

2. Necesito comprar algo para la fiesta.

   ____

3. Diana va de compras y yo voy también.

   ____

4. No hay nadie en clase con una corbata.

   ____

5. No me gusta ningún pantalón en la tienda.

   ____

6. No voy a comprar ni una camisa ni unos zapatos.

   ____

15 Yesterday Marta had a great day shopping in Panama, and she summarizes it below. Choose verbs from the list provided and then conjugate them in the preterite tense to complete her narration. You will use each verb once.

ir	pedir	preferir	ser	comprar

No voy de compras mucho pero ayer yo (1) ______________ a muchas tiendas en la Ciudad de Panamá con mi amigo Luis. (2) ¡______________ un día fantástico y nosotros (3) ______________ mucha ropa. Yo (4) ______________ comprar ropa para la playa porque aquí hace mucho calor. Más tarde en un restaurante nosotros (5) ______________ café y un postre muy bueno.

Nombre: ______________________ Fecha: ____________

Lección B

1 Imagine that you have just bought presents for family members and friends. For each present listed, identify the recipient and explain your gift selection.

MODELO: el paraguas
El paraguas es para mi tía porque llueve mucho en su ciudad.

1. el perfume
____
2. la billetera
____
3. el pijama
____
4. el cinturón
____
5. la bufanda
____
6. la pulsera de oro
____

2 Make a list of five presents you received in the past year. Then note the occasion for the present, the person who gave it to you and your reaction.

	El regalo	¿Por qué?	¿De quién?	Mi reacción
MODELO:	un suéter	mi cumpleaños	mi abuela	¡qué bonito!
1.				
2.				
3.				
4.				
5.				

Nombre: ______________________ Fecha: __________

3 Answer the following questions in complete sentences.

1. ¿Prefieres dar o recibir regalos?

____

____

2. ¿A quién le das regalos con frecuencia?

____

____

3. ¿Quién te da regalos con frecuencia?

____

____

4. ¿En qué tienda buscas regalos especiales?

____

____

5. ¿En qué ocasión especial te gusta dar regalos?

____

____

Nombre: ______________________ Fecha: ______________

Repaso rápido: Diminutives

Remember that to indicate affection or convey the idea that something is small you should replace the final vowel of a noun with the endings *-ito, -ita, -itos* and *-itas: Clara (Clarita).* For nouns that end in a consonant, add the endings *-cito, -cita, -citos* or *-citas* to the complete word: *cinturón (cinturoncito).* Additional diminutive endings you may encounter include *-illo, -illa, -uelo, -uela, -ico* and *-ica.* Other words may require a spelling change: *poquito (poco).*

4 Give the diminutives of the following names.

MODELO: Belén → Belencita

1. Julio → ______________
2. Sara → ______________
3. Adolfo → ______________
4. Gloria → ______________
5. Roberto → ______________
6. Elena → ______________
7. Javier → ______________
8. Rosario → ______________

Nombre: ______________________ Fecha: ____________

Repaso rápido: Preterite tense of *leer, oír, ver, decir, hacer* and *tener*

leer		**oír**		**ver**	
leí	leímos	oí	oímos	vi	vimos
leíste	leísteis	oíste	oísteis	viste	visteis
leyó	leyeron	oyó	oyeron	vio	vieron

decir		**hacer**		**tener**	
dije	dijimos	hice	hicimos	tuve	tuvimos
dijiste	dijisteis	hiciste	hicisteis	tuviste	tuvisteis
dijo	dijeron	hizo	hicieron	tuvo	tuvieron

5 Combine items from each column to say what different people did yesterday.

mi amiga	leer	un programa de televisión
mi amiga y yo	oír	un programa de radio
yo	ver	un examen importante
mis abuelos	decir	un postre especial
el/la profesor(a)	hacer	un partido de béisbol
tú	tener	una revista interesante
Ud.		las noticias

1. ______________________________
2. ______________________________
3. ______________________________
4. ______________________________
5. ______________________________
6. ______________________________
7. ______________________________

Nombre: ______________________________ Fecha: ______________

6 Complete the crossword puzzle with the appropriate preterite tense of the conjugations indicated.

Horizontales

2. yo (tener)
4. nosotros (ver)
6. yo (hacer)
7. tú (leer)
8. yo (oír)
9. ellos (decir)
10. ella (oír)
11. ellos (ver)

Verticales

1. tú (tener)
2. nosotros (tener)
3. ellas (hacer)
5. ellos (leer)
6. ella (hacer)
9. yo (decir)

Nombre: ______________________________ Fecha: ______________

7 Write what you and your friends did yesterday, using the preterite forms of the indicated verbs.

MODELO: Graciela / hacer una paella con su prima
Graciela hizo una paella con su prima.

1. Pedro / oír música en su computadora portátil

____

2. Rafael y Soledad / ver la nueva película de Penélope Cruz

____

3. Uds. / no hacer nada

____

4. yo / leer una revista de tecnología

____

5. tú / tener que ir al médico

____

6. todos mis amigos / oír música por Internet en mi casa

____

7. María y Edgar / decir muchas cosas a Humberto

____

Nombre: ______________________________ Fecha: ______________

8 Answer the following questions about last week.

1. ¿Qué libros leíste para tus clases?

____

2. ¿Qué programa de televisión o película viste?

____

3. ¿Qué hiciste en tu tiempo libre?

____

4. ¿Qué hicieron tus amigos el viernes?

____

5. ¿Qué tuviste que hacer en tu casa?

____

6. ¿Qué tuvieron que hacer las otras personas en tu familia?

____

9 Find seven shopping terms that are spelled out in the grid.

T	O	Í	P	E	A	U	É	C	A	X	B
P	A	G	A	R	N	L	I	A	I	Ú	A
I	H	B	Ó	P	F	T	Y	J	O	T	R
L	O	F	E	R	T	A	B	A	M	P	A
P	R	O	M	A	Y	D	Ó	N	I	J	T
C	R	É	D	I	T	O	F	R	É	D	O
Q	A	C	A	L	I	D	A	D	P	I	Y
T	R	O	Ú	B	V	O	P	Z	C	V	I

Nombre: ______________________ Fecha: __________

10 Choose from the list provided to write the expression that corresponds to each definition.

pagar en efectivo	las ofertas	el cambio
la tarjeta de crédito	el dependiente	el recibo

1. El hombre que trabaja en la caja y ayuda a los clientes. ______________________
2. Es de plástico y sirve para comprar. ______________________
3. El documento de la compra; puede ser papel o electrónico. ______________________
4. Cuando hay precios especiales en las tiendas. ______________________
5. Pagar con dinero y no con la tarjeta de crédito. ______________________
6. El dinero que a veces recibes después de pagar en efectivo. ______________________

11 Answer the following questions about your shopping habits.

1. ¿Dónde te gusta ir de compras?

   ____
2. ¿Cuándo hay ofertas especiales?

   ____
3. ¿Prefieres pagar en efectivo o a crédito?

   ____
4. ¿Es más importante el buen precio o la buena calidad?

   ____
5. ¿Qué tienda tiene buenos precios y buena calidad?

   ____
6. ¿Qué tienda tiene precios caros y buena calidad?

   ____

Nombre: ______________________________ Fecha: ______________

Repaso rápido: Using prepositions

You have learned the following prepositions in Spanish:

a	de	en	para	sin
con	desde	hasta	por	sobre

You also have learned that prepositions are sometimes accompanied by prepositional pronouns. For example, with the verb *gustar* you have used prepositional pronouns in combination with the preposition *a* for clarity or emphasis.

__A ella__ le gusta pagar con la tarjeta de crédito.
__A nosotros__ nos gusta pagar en efectivo.

The following prepositional pronouns may be used with the prepositions you have learned:

para **mí**	para **nosotros/as**
para **ti**	para **vosotros/as**
para **Ud.**	para **Uds.**
para **él**	para **ellos**
para **ella**	para **ellas**

Two exceptions are *conmigo* (with me) and *contigo* (with you), which are used with the preposition *con* instead of *mí* and *ti*.

¿Vas a ir conmigo a la tienda?
Sí, voy a ir contigo.

12 Complete each of the following sentences with an appropriate preposition.

1. Compro un bolso ______________ mi hermana.
2. Siempre debes ir a las fiestas ______________ tu hermano.
3. Pones los vasos sucios ______________ el lavaplatos.
4. ¿______________ ti te gusta comprar perfumes?
5. Voy ______________ el centro comercial y vuelvo.
6. La pulsera de oro está ______________ la mesa de la cocina.
7. El cinturón es ______________ cuero.
8. Clara va a tu casa ______________ la noche.

Nombre: ______________________________ Fecha: ______________

13 Complete each sentence by providing the logical word.

MODELO: Es el cumpleaños de Alicia. Este regalo es para ella.

1. Es el aniversario de mis abuelos. Este regalo es para ______________.
2. Paco está muy triste. Yo debo hablar con ______________ para saber cuál es el problema.
3. A Juan le gusta la tienda de música. También nos gusta mucho a ______________.
4. Tú piensas ir al partido y yo también quiero ir. Voy a ir al partido ______________.
5. Lola está enferma. Ramón no tiene ganas de ir al cine sin ______________.
6. Tú y yo acabamos de terminar la tarea. ¿Quieres ir al cine ______________?

14 Answer the following questions negatively, using the given cues.

MODELO: ¿Es la corbata para Juan? (Ramiro)
No, no es para él. Es para Ramiro.

1. ¿Es el collar de perlas para Rosa? (Sofía)

____

2. ¿Son los pañuelos para Gloria y Teresa? (Amparo)

____

3. ¿Son los aretes de plata para mí? (Marta)

____

4. ¿Son los pijamas para Javier y Carlos? (tú)

____

5. ¿Son los relojes para nosotros? (Alfredo y Graciela)

____

6. ¿Son las billeteras para Elena y Alfonso? (tú y yo)

____

Nombre: ______________________________ Fecha: ______________

Unidad 10

Lección A

1 Choose from the following activities to summarize what you and others did last weekend.

ir de compras	trabajar	bailar
estudiar mucho	leer una revista	ir al teatro
montar en bicicleta	limpiar la casa	escribir una carta
comer en un restaurante	preparar la comida	ver televisión

MODELO: El domingo preparé la comida para mi familia.

1. ______________________________

2. ______________________________

3. ______________________________

4. ______________________________

5. ______________________________

6. ______________________________

7. ______________________________

8. ______________________________

Nombre: ______________________ Fecha: ____________

2 Interview your classmates to find out who did the following things last weekend. You should find a different person for each activity.

Actividad	**Nombre**
estudiar mucho	______
leer una revista	______
ver una película	______
ir de compras	______
montar en bicicleta	______
limpiar la casa	______
escribir una carta	______
trabajar	______
comer en un restaurante	______
cocinar	______
ir a un concierto	______
dormir muchas horas	______

3 Find eight school subjects that are spelled out in the grid.

A	R	T	E	X	A	E	É	M	A	X	B
P	A	G	Á	H	I	S	T	Ú	I	U	I
Í	H	B	O	P	F	P	Y	S	O	T	O
C	O	M	P	U	T	A	C	I	Ó	N	L
P	R	O	M	A	Y	Ñ	Ó	C	I	J	O
I	N	G	L	É	S	O	F	A	E	D	G
Q	A	C	A	L	I	L	A	D	P	I	Í
T	R	Ó	U	H	I	S	T	O	R	I	A
M	A	T	E	M	Á	T	I	C	A	S	C

Nombre: ______________________________ Fecha: ______________

4 Answer the following questions to note what you and others have to do in the next few days.

1. ¿Qué tienes que hacer esta noche?

   ____

2. ¿Qué tienes que hacer mañana?

   ____

3. ¿Qué tienes que hacer el próximo fin de semana?

   ____

4. ¿Qué tienen que hacer tus amigos?

   ____

5. ¿Qué tiene que hacer tu mejor amiga?

   ____

6. ¿Qué tienen que hacer los profesores?

   ____

5 Answer the following questions about your life at school.

1. ¿Cuáles son tus clases favoritas?

   ____

2. ¿Por qué te gustan estas clases?

   ____

3. ¿En qué clases tienes que trabajar mucho?

   ____

4. ¿Qué te gusta de la escuela?

   ____

5. ¿En qué deportes o clubes participas?

   ____

6. ¿Cuándo terminas la escuela este año?

   ____

Nombre: ______________________________ Fecha: ______________

6 Use the verb *gustar* and provide additional information to summarize what you especially liked and disliked about the school year that will soon be over.

1. Me gustó mucho ______________________________.
2. Me gustaron mucho ______________________________.
3. Me gustó ______________________________.
4. Me gustaron ______________________________.
5. No me gustó ______________________________.
6. No me gustaron ______________________________.

7 Write a composition in Spanish about the school year that is about to end. Include information about your activities, classes, friends and special events.

____

____

____

____

____

____

____

____

____

____

____

____

Nombre: ______________________________ Fecha: ______________

Lección B

1 The words in the box below indicate places in the Spanish-speaking world that you have learned about this year. Refer to them as you complete the following statements about your travel interests.

México	Puerto Rico	Nicaragua
Colombia	Ecuador	
Venezuela	Argentina	Chile
España	Panamá	República Dominicana
Perú	Guatemala	
Costa Rica	Bolivia	Uruguay

1. Me gustaría visitar ______________________ porque ______________________ ____.
2. Me gustaría viajar a ______________________. En este país yo ______________________ ____.
3. También me gustaría visitar ______________________ porque ______________________ ____.
4. En ______________________ me gustaría ______________________ ____.
5. ______________________ me parece muy interesante. En este país yo ____.

Nombre: ______________________________ Fecha: ______________

2 Answer the following questions about your plans for the summer.

1. ¿Qué piensas hacer durante las vacaciones?

____

____

2. ¿Vas a viajar a algún lugar interesante?

____

____

3. ¿Tienes que trabajar durante el verano?

____

____

4. ¿Qué trabajo te gustaría hacer?

____

____

5. ¿Piensas ir a un concierto especial?

____

____

6. ¿Qué deportes vas a jugar?

____

____

7. ¿Quién va a celebrar tu cumpleaños durante el verano?

____

____

Nombre: ______________________________ Fecha: ______________

3 Complete the following crossword puzzle of jobs you can do during the summer.

Horizontales

2. trabajar en una tienda como __
5. trabajar en una __ como secretario/a
7. __ casas sucias
8. cuidar __

Verticales

1. trabajar de __ en un restaurante
3. hacer __ de jardinería
4. ser salvavidas de una __
6. reparar __

Nombre: ______________________________ Fecha: ______________

4 Write an e-mail to a friend in a Spanish-speaking country. In your e-mail include information about your activities, school, family and plans for vacation.

Nombre: ______________________ Fecha: __________

5 List five of your favorite activities for each season of the year in order of preference.

verano

1. ______________________
2. ______________________
3. ______________________
4. ______________________
5. ______________________

otoño

1. ______________________
2. ______________________
3. ______________________
4. ______________________
5. ______________________

invierno

1. ______________________
2. ______________________
3. ______________________
4. ______________________
5. ______________________

primavera

1. ______________________
2. ______________________
3. ______________________
4. ______________________
5. ______________________

Nombre: ______________________________ Fecha: ______________

6 Find nine professions that are spelled out in the grid.

S	G	H	J	K	Q	W	Ó	I	K	L	Q	W	É	R
D	F	J	H	L	Á	E	P	U	O	Z	I	U	Y	T
A	G	R	I	C	U	L	T	O	R	X	Ó	P	L	K
R	D	K	G	Z	S	R	L	Y	E	C	G	H	J	P
Q	S	L	F	X	D	T	K	T	U	V	F	D	S	R
U	A	M	É	D	I	C	O	R	Q	B	W	Q	A	O
I	C	P	D	C	F	Y	A	M	N	Ñ	E	R	T	G
T	V	O	S	V	G	T	J	E	A	M	I	Ú	Y	R
E	E	Í	A	B	S	Ú	H	W	B	E	O	P	A	A
C	K	U	Q	I	H	I	G	Q	J	S	S	D	F	M
T	V	E	T	E	R	N	A	R	I	O	H	T	G	A
O	B	R	W	Ñ	J	O	F	Á	H	J	K	L	R	D
G	A	Y	E	O	K	P	D	S	G	Z	X	C	V	O
W	F	T	R	M	L	A	S	D	F	Q	M	N	B	R
Í	R	C	O	C	I	N	E	R	O	W	É	R	T	Y

7 In the left column list five careers that interest you. Then explain why you find each one appealing.

	Carrera	**¿Por qué?**
MODELO:	médico/a	Me gusta ayudar a otras personas.
1.	________________	______________________________
2.	________________	______________________________
3.	________________	______________________________
4.	________________	______________________________
5.	________________	______________________________